RENTAL
PROPERTY
INVESTING &
PASSIVE
INCOME

THE HOLY GRAIL OF
FINANCIAL FREEDOM

JONATHAN FITZPATRICK

RENTAL PROPERTY INVESTING & PASSIVE INCOME
THE HOLY GRAIL OF FINANCIAL FREEDOM
Copyright © 2019 by Jonathan Fitzpatrick.

For information contact :
Suite #K231125
13820 NE Airport Way
Portland, OR, 97251
United States

www.jonathanfitzpatrickauthor.com
info@jonathanfitzpatrickauthor.com
www.facebook.com/jonathanfitzpatrickauthor

First Edition : November 2019

DISCLAIMER

The information contained in this book is for general information and educational purposes only. This book assumes no responsibility for errors or omissions in the contents on the Service.

This book have no liability for any damage or loss (including, without limitation, financial loss, loss of profits, loss of business or any indirect or consequential loss).

JONATHAN FITZPATRICK

SIGN UP!

Visit our website:

WWW.JONATHANFITZPATRICKAUTHOR.COM

and enter you email address to receive exclusive bonus contents related to the updates of this book and find out everything about Jonathan Fitzpatrick's new publications, launch offers and other exclusive promotions!

CONTENTS

RENTAL PROPERTY INVESTING

SECRETS OF A REAL ESTATE BUILDING EMPIRE

Principles to Make 7 Figures of a Passive Income
Establishing a Real Estate Investment Empire

JONATHAN FITZPATRICK

INTRODUCTION

You can be your own boss and pay yourself from the profits of the business!

Have you ever dreamed of off for a week's vacation and not have to get permission from the boss? Have you ever wanted to take a day off for no particular reason and just do nothing? Well, I can and I want to show you how to do it, too.

I am Jonathan Fitzpatrick and I am my own boss. I started my entrepreneurial career online with a business called Amazon FBA. My life has completely changed in just twelve short months. Thanks to this online business, I was able to quit my day job and work for myself. Eventually, I reached a net profit level in the six-figure range and I stabilized there. I can give you all the details of my success in *Amazon FBA Mastery Coaching: The Definitive Guide to Learn the Secret Way to Sell Fulfillment by Amazon* which is available at Amazon.com.

But while I was more than pleased with my success, I realized that I needed to differentiate my business in order to continue to grow my financial security the way I wanted to. This is a fundamental requirement for continued growth and development. I needed another source of passive income because economic stability depends on having multiple sources of income.

After researching several opportunities, I knew that real estate investing would give me the perfect opportunity to continue to grow my wealth. I soon learned that even though I already have a six-figure income, it would not be needed for me to invest in real estate. I found so many ways to begin my career with little or no money down.

You will find many options available in the real estate market—opportunities that will give you a regular source of income for years to come. With the proper tools and techniques, which I intend to give you, you will be able to enjoy the exact same kind of success that I am currently enjoying in my life. With this knowledge, the only other thing you will need is to have a positive mindset and be prepared to succeed. This book is about the correct way to buy and maintain rental real estate properties. There is the right way and the wrong way to do it, just like any other field. I want to show you the right way to make money in this field. You can't just find a listing and assume it will be perfect. But there are ways to find good listings and this book will show you how to do it. This book will show you what a good rental property is, how to find it, and how to get it. And yes, there are ways to acquire property even if you don't have down payment money available or if you already have multiple mortgages on the books. Anything is possible. I will show you through my experiences how to be successful in the rental real estate market.

Successful real estate investing will give you everything you need to achieve present and future financial security. You will learn the basic of the business and what you need to know to grow your own empire and enjoy the same success that I am currently enjoying. You will learn how to overcome challenges and be able to anticipate issues that you can easily avoid on your path to success.

Be prepared to be excited and energized by what you will see in this book. This book will fill you with knowledge and excitement and everything you need to be successful in the rental property real estate market.

So let's get started.

CHAPTER
ONE

1. REASONS TO INVEST IN REAL ESTATE RENTAL PROPERTY

You will quickly learn how much I love the world of rental property real estate. Since I have discovered how easy it is to make money at this and how much fun it actually is, I really don't want to stop. I originally got into this business as an addition to my portfolio. I was already enjoying success with my Amazon online business but I knew I needed to diversify if I wanted to keep growing my wealth and my future possibilities. So I chose real estate rental property.

There are many reasons someone might choose this field as one in which they can make money—now and in the future. One of the most important reasons, at least in the beginning, is that you can start with one rental property while you continue to work at your regular job. Because let's be honest; most people can't just quit their day job the moment they buy their first rental property. Getting into the market this way will mean that you will need to work nights and weekends on the rental property but if it is a necessary way to get started, then that is what you will do.

Once you have several properties and you are enjoying regular cash flow then you might be able to drop down to part-time or to quit altogether. Be patient; it will happen.

The real estate market is relatively easy to learn and that includes rental property investing. There are many available resources, both in the library and online, that will give you the answer to any question you might have. There are many people who are more than willing to share the things they have learned with those who are just starting out.

Buying rental property allows you to manage your monetary investment directly if you chose to. Some people will hire a property manager but if this is your full-time job and you want to be a hands-on kind of landlord, this is the business to do it in. And if you enjoy being in charge and controlling events, then rental property is the market for you because you are responsible directly for what happens to your investment. It is your responsibility to check out the property before you buy it to make sure it is a good investment. It is your job to make certain the property is suitable for and attractive to potential renters. The preferred way for many people to do this is to manage the business themselves.

Of all the things that people can give up in life, people will always need somewhere to live. Not everyone can afford to become a homeowner because even if they have the down payment, they may not have the income to be able to afford the regular upkeep of a house. Not everyone wants to be a homeowner. For whatever reason you can think of, there will always be people who need to rent somewhere to live. And you can provide this place.

Rental property is real; it is a tangible investment. You can see it right in front of you. If you make an improvement on the property, then you can see how much better it looks afterward. Rental property may occasionally drop in value but it will always come back up and while it is rented to someone you will continue to make money. And you can use other people's money to grow your investments. Other people will help with down payments. Other people will pay you rent money to live in your house.

And along with the nearly constant cash flow, you will also enjoy tax breaks as the owner of rental property. There are many tax laws that make a favorable environment for property owners. For instance, the interest expense that you pay along with your monthly mortgage payment is tax deductible. Your operating expenses are also deductible. This means that your depreciation, insurance, property taxes, and operating expenses are all deductible. This is an extra layer of savings that will be much enjoyed at tax time.

Buying real estate to use as rental property is a fantastic investment if you are willing to do what you need to do to be successful. You will get amazing returns if you just learn the processes. The best thing about rental property is that they become better investments the longer that you own them. You make cash flow from rental properties every month, money that comes to you on a regular basis. Your cash flow will naturally increase over time because the rate of rental payments will increase but your mortgage payment will remain steady, thus making your cash flow increase on a regular basis. When the mortgage is paid off the cash flow will significantly increase.

And by purchasing rental property you are building equity for your future, including money for your retirement. The monetary difference between what you owe and what the house is worth is the equity. Since the value of the property will increase over time as the amount that you owe becomes less, your equity is always increasing. And once the properties are paid off, the rental income will provide a nice regular source of income for your later years.

Investing in rental property has many overall benefits and will prove to be a great source for passive income. Your potential for profit will increase because the value of rental property increases with the increasing demand for property. There are several important advantages to investing in real estate for rental property. As long as you go into this with your eyes wide open and a ready mindset, you will be successful.

CHAPTER

TWO

2. FINDING PROPERTY FOR RENTAL UNITS

Investors are able to find rental properties that are available for sale by using many different techniques. If you rely on a wide variety of resources to help you find properties, then you will be giving yourself the best overall possible chance to find the investment property that is perfect for you.

Networking is one way that many people use to find rental properties. This method will give you access to properties that the general public may not know about yet. People are often hearing about their friends and neighbors who are thinking about selling their homes. This could give you the inside track on a new property to purchase. Professional contacts such as attorneys or contractors might also have information regarding other properties for sale.

Some people prefer to join investment clubs that are groups of people who spend their time looking for and talking about real estate. These clubs may have a small annual membership fee of a few hundred dollars but that can be well worth it for the chance to find new properties to buy.

And the membership fee is most likely tax deductible as a business expense. You might also belong to a group of other property investors or landlords who will hear about available properties that they themselves might not be interested in.

Realtors are a great source of information regarding properties to buy for rental properties. After all, the realtor's job is to locate properties for sale for people who want to buy them and to locate people to buy the properties their clients want to sell. You can easily make an appointment with a realtor to look at individual listings. Or you can drive through a particular area that you might want to own property in to see if any properties are for sale. If you find any, you can call the realtor listed on the sign and make an appointment to see the house. You can also check out open houses where you can actually go through the house and look at it with less intimate contact with the realtor since hopefully many people will be viewing the house at the same time you are.

Banks often have a backlog of properties available that are for sale because they have been foreclosed on. Banks like to sell these properties because they do not bring in any income for the bank sitting empty and unused. These properties are generally listed with a realtor eventually but if you can catch a listing before it goes to the realtor then you can avoid paying the realtor's fees and this will save you money.

Do not overlook the newspaper as a valuable source of information. Many people get their news online these days but there are certain things that will still be found in the newspaper in black and white print. In the classified section you will find notices of foreclosures or sheriff's sales. A foreclosure sale is held when a lending institution has reacquired a property from an owner who could not or did not make their monthly mortgage payment. The lender will take allow all interested people to tour the property and then they will take bids for buying the property, either during a live auction or by sealed bid. The bidder with the best bid wins. These properties are generally sold for the value of the note owing on the house so it is possible to pick up a good property for less money. These are sometimes referred to as sheriff's sales. These will be listed in the newspaper because they must be publicly announced.

Buying property at a foreclosure sale or a sheriff's sale is a great way to find a good deal on a property for investment purposes. These are local sales held by the county government. These sales are open to the public. Anyone who wants to bid on a property must have the funds in place prior to the sale and you must have proof that the funds are available. Property listings, either online or in the newspaper, will include the address and description of the property and the listing will also include the upset price. This is the minimum amount that the plaintiff (the one who is selling the property) will take as a bid for the property. It is a good idea to do a complete coverage title search on any property you might want to buy. Searching the title for discrepancies will tell you if there are any liens against the house, such as contractor liens, utility company liens, or even liens from any source that collects tax money. Liens are lawsuits placed on a property when that particular bill has not been paid by the homeowner. So if you hire someone to put new gutters on your house and you never pay him, he can file a lien against your property. These liens may or may not be satisfied (paid off) by the proceeds from the sale. If they are not, then the new owner is responsible for paying them.

The amount of money that you bid on a property depends on two things: how much is the minimum required bid and how much are you willing to spend. You must bring a certified check, also known as a cashier's check or an official check, for the down payment. You will need to know what percentage of the purchase price the down payment must be. It might be ten percent, fifteen percent, or twenty percent. So if you are willing to pay at the most $200,000 for the property then you must bring a check for twenty thousand dollars on a ten percent down, thirty thousand dollars on a fifteen percent down, and forty thousand dollars on a twenty percent down. Closing depends on the term of the local county sheriff's office but it is usually within thirty days. That means in thirty days from the auction you must have your financing arranged and have taken possession of the house.

When you are ready to buy your first property you need to decide what your personal criteria will be for the property. Making this list is like making a shopping list for the grocery store. Deciding before your search exactly what you are looking for will help keep you focused on the search so that you will be able to find the kind of properties that you are looking for. When you are making your list be sure to think about all of the attributes you would like a house to have. If you are in a large city and looking in the suburbs, which city would you prefer? Which neighborhood would you like to buy into? How big will the lot be and how many square feet will be in the house. Do you want to buy move-in ready or a fixer-upper? What is the CAP rate? How much cash flow can you expect to receive? What is the potential for appreciation?

CAP rate refers to the term capitalization rate, which is the amount of money you would expect to receive from a property over the period of one year. It will help you to determine whether or not a particular property is a good investment. The CAP rate is the ratio of property asset value to net operating income. So let's say you are looking at two different properties that are already set up as rental units. Both properties are rented for ninety-five percent of the year.

Property A	Property B
Value $500,000	Value $600,000
Occupancy rate 95%	Occupancy rate 95%
Gross rental income $60,000	Gross rental income $72,000
Operating expenses $25,000	Operating expenses $32,000

The first step in the equation is to multiply the gross rental income by the occupancy rate:

Property A: 95% x $60,000 = $57,000
Property B: 95% x $72,000 = $68,400

The next step is to subtract the operating expenses:

Property A: $57,000 - $25,000 = $32,000
Property B: $68,400 - $32,000 = $36,400

Now you have the Net Operating Income (NOI). This is the yearly income that is generated by a rental property counting all of the income that is generated from operations and subtracting the expenses that come from operating the property. Divide the NOI number by the current value of the property to get the CAP rate:

Property A: $32,000/$500,000 = 0.064
Property B: $36,400/$600,000 = 0.060

Since the CAP rate is always expressed as a percentage, now multiply each number by one hundred:

Property A: 0.064 x 100 = 6.4% CAP rate
Property B: 0.060 x 100 = 6% CAP rate

These two properties have a similar CAP rate. The determining factor in this example would be some other consideration, such as sales price or location. The figures for the operating expenses, rental income, and occupancy rate can be obtained from the realtor.

An acceptable CAP rate falls somewhere between four percent and ten percent. The CAP rate should just be used as an indicator of profitability while considering other factors. Obviously if the CAP rate falls out of these percentages then the property might not make you the money you desire. You also need to consider local demand, inventory that is available in the area, and the type of property this one is specifically. As an example, a CAP rate of four percent might be quite normal in areas of high demand such as New York City and California. But in an area where the demand is lower, such as an area that is going through regeneration or in a rural area, the normal CAP rate might be ten percent or even higher.

Most buyers look for a higher CAP rate, which means the price to purchase the property is rather low when compared to the net operating income. Unfortunately, a lower CAP rate usually represents a lower risk property where a higher CAP rate usually means a property with a higher risk. A property that has a higher CAP rate might be located in an area that doesn't have much opportunity for regular rental increases or where property does not appreciate as well as it does in other areas. As an investor you will need to weigh all of these factors when deciding on a property to purchase.

One thing to remember when comparing CAP rates is to compare rates on similar properties. This just means to compare properties that are similar to each other and are in similar areas. An investment property that is a multifamily rental unit will probably have a CAP rate that is much lower than a commercial building that is full of retail tenants. This means that the multifamily unit will probably be an investment of lower reward than the commercial building but it will also probably be a lower risk. This is because in times of economic downturn people still need to live somewhere, where retail customers might close up and move away.

CAP rates are affected by four factors:

2.1 INTEREST RATES

Property values typically fall when interest rates rise. When the rates rise, the debt ratio usually rises which will mean a decrease in net cash flow so lower CAP rates come from rising interest rates. The rent will remain the same but if the interest rate is higher then you will not make as large of a profit.

2.2 AVAILABLE INVENTORY

This term refers to the number of properties that are available in one particular area. If the inventory is lower the demand for property will be higher, this will lead to properties with a lower CAP rate.

2.3 ASSET CLASS

This is the factor that tells what type of property it is, like a commercial property, a single-family dwelling, an apartment building, etc. Residential properties usually have lower CAP rates than commercial properties because you can charge a higher rent to a commercial tenant.

2.4 LOCATION

The local economy and property demand is driven by the location of the property. A property in a more desirable location will have a higher value and higher rents, which will affect the overall CAP rate.

CAP rate is only one way to evaluate properties when deciding which property is the better investment. You should really be prepared to consider several factors when deciding which property will be the best investment property for you to buy. Doing this will give you a better, more well-rounded picture of the property and whether it has a reasonable potential to be a good investment for you. Particularly if the property needs to be remodeled or is vacant you will probably want to use extra tools in order to evaluate it. Here are several ways to make an evaluation of a potential investment property:

2.4.1 RETURN ON INVESTMENT (ROI)

Usually ten percent or more is considered to be a good ROI for any real estate investment property. ROI is determined by dividing your total investment into your annual return. Annual return is determined by subtracting the amount of expenses from the total rental income.

2.4.2 THE PERCENTAGE RULE

This is the one percent rule or the two percent rule, both are used equally. This guide says that the monthly gross income should be at least one percent, or two percent, of the price of the purchase. If the monthly gross income is more than one percent of the price of the purchase, then the property usually will have a positive flow of cash.

2.4.3 GROSS RENTAL YIELD

Take the collected annual rent by the total cost of the property and then multiply by one hundred; the higher the number the better the yield. The total cost of the property will include any renovation costs, closing costs, and the purchase price.

2.4.4 CASH FLOW

See if the expected monthly rental income covers the monthly costs that will include the homeowner's association fees, utilities, taxes, insurance, and mortgage payment. If the rental amount collected exceeds the amount of expenses, then the cash flow is positive.

2.4.5 PER-UNIT PRICE

In a multifamily unit or a commercial building take the purchase price and divide it by the number of units in the building. This will give you a price per unit so that you can determine if the unit is worth that price based on its cosmetic appearance and overall usefulness.

2.4.6 COMPARABLE PROPERTIES

Get the figures from the last three to six months of the sale price, rental rates, and occupancy rates for buildings that are similar to the building you are considering purchasing. When comparing properties, they need to be similar in size, have amenities that are similar, and be the same types of properties.

When considering the other factors that are listed on your particular list of criteria, remember that you have the right to be as demanding as you want to be. No one can tell you what your particular investment should look like. Just remember that if you are too narrow in your consideration, you might not have very much inventory to choose from. But when you are able to specify the particular criteria of the rental property, you want to own it will be easy for you to search for a property to buy. And in knowing what you want to buy you will be better able to tell other people what you are looking for. Just telling people "Hey, I'm looking for rental properties to buy" will probably get you a nice smile. But telling people "Hey, I'm looking for a three-bedroom, two bath, single family home on a one-acre lot in the Millwood are of town" will probably get you some action on your request.

The most important part of the package of criteria that you will assemble is the financial part of your package. If the financial component of the deal does not add up to a profit, that property will probably not be a good deal. Usually a real estate listing will not tell you the information that you might find important to know about the financial information of a property. While you might be able to calculate an estimation for the amount of rental income a property might bring in, you will not immediately know how much cash flow the property brings in every month, if the property is overpriced, or exactly how much you should offer on the property. And even though you might love working a spreadsheet, it will not make sense to work one up for each property you are looking at. This is when you learn to use the "rules."

The 'rules' comes from the term "rules of thumb." These rules will give a buyer a rapid way to evaluate the financial health of a property. Using these rules is not exact and should not be the only consideration used to determine the worth of a property. These rules can help you quickly decide if a property may or may not be worth pursuing.

We have already discussed the one percent or two percent, rule. This rule is that whichever percent you use the monthly rental income should be that percentage of the purchase price. So using this rule a house that is priced at $100,000 should bring either $1000 or $2000 in rent each month. This is a very simple way to compare properties but it can let you know whether or not a particular property needs more investigation. Using the rule from the other way works like this: if the monthly rent is $500, you would not pay more than $50,000 for the house at the rate of one percent.

Then there is the fifty percent rule. This rule will help you to somewhat accurately tell how much your monthly expenses will be on the property. This rule is that fifty percent of your monthly income will be used for expenses on the property and this does not include the monthly mortgage payment. Since most real estate listings will tell you how much monthly income comes from the property you can easily get a good estimate of your monthly cash flow. Take the monthly income and divide that number in half. So half will go to expense and the other half needs to be enough to cover the mortgage. Anything left over is cash flow. The fifty percent for expenses will need to cover rehab costs for tenant turnover, management costs, utilities, vacancies, taxes, insurance, repairs, and some savings for the larger cost items like repaving or a new roof.

The last rule that is often used is the seventy percent rule. This rule is used by investors to determine quickly the maximum amount of the purchase price that you should offer. This number is based on the after-repair value (ARV) of the property and is used for those properties that will require a major renovation before they are ready to rent. This rule says you should pay no more than seventy percent of the value of the property after repairs minus the costs of the repairs. Use the following as an example:

This property needs extensive repair before it can be rented. After renovation it should sell for about two hundred thousand dollars. It needs around thirty-five thousand dollars in repair work. So to use the seventy percent rule you would multiply two hundred thousand by seventy percent to get one hundred forty thousand and then subtract the thirty-five thousand for the repair costs. That means the most you should pay for this property would be one hundred five thousand dollars.

Keep in mind that the rules of them are only used to give an efficient and quick way to screen a property. Any property that falls far out of line of one of the rules is probably not worth investing any more time or attention and especially not money.

When you are ready to buy a property, you will certainly not hand over a check and get keys in return. It does not work as quickly as it seems to work on television. There is a set process that is followed every time you purchase a property, no matter what type of property it is.

So let's begin at the point where you have found the property you want and you are ready to buy it. Your very first step is to decide how you are going to finance this purchase. This just means that you already have in mind a definite idea of how you are going to pay for this property. You need to be pre-approved by the lender if you are going to use a loan from any financial institution. If you have the funds and want to do an all cash offer, then those funds need to be liquid and available immediately. Liquid means they are sitting in a bank account or a credit union account and you can walk in the door and get an official check for the amount you need. If you are planning to use the proceeds from the sale of the jewelry Aunt Martha left you in her will, then that jewelry needs to have been already sold and the money put into an account. Money is liquid, property is an asset. Most real estate agents as well as anyone who has been buying real estate for any length of time, will recommend that you have your financing in place first before you ever go looking for property. If you find a great deal the chances are good that someone else found that same great deal, and whoever brings the money to the table first wins. So have your choice of financing ready.

Now you want you make an offer. This offer is made on paper, usually on a pre-printed form that has all of the correct legal terms on it. You will also determine the amount of time the offer will be good for. You and your real estate agent (if you are using one) will simply fill in the blanks and then it will go to the seller or their real estate agent. The seller's real estate agent will take it to their client and together they will discuss the offer and determine if it is acceptable to them. If you are not using an agent, you can find appropriate forms online but have your attorney look over the form before you submit it to make sure there are no errors.

When making an offer you do not need to offer the sale price. Perhaps the property needs renovation and the seventy percent rule calculations you did came up with a purchase price lower than what the seller is asking for. Sometimes sellers will ask for a price higher than what the property is worth to see how much they can get. It is perfectly acceptable to offer less than the sales price. Also, in your offer you will put any contingencies that you have. These are stipulations that must occur before you will agree to buy the property. You may require any number of contingencies in the offer:

2.5 HOME INSPECTION

This will allow you to hire a home inspector who is certified by your state to do home inspections. While home inspectors can't possibly see all the problems a property might have, they can certainly see problems that might cause a hefty repair bill like the need for foundation work or a new work.

2.6 FINANCING

If you have not already arranged financing this clause should be put in.

2.7 APPRAISAL

This one states that if the appraisal on the house is not as high as the offer then the offer is voided. You can also stipulate that the seller has the option of lowering the sale price to meet the appraisal amount. The appraisal is the lending company's expert opinion of the value of the property. The lender will not lend money over the appraised value of the house.

2.8 INSURANCE

This clause gives you time to make certain that the home is able to be insured for an amount that you are willing to pay. Certain things will dramatically increase the price of homeowner's insurance, such as if the property is in a flood plain or a zone that is prone to earthquakes. Maybe the house has mold or has had mold in the past. All of these will either increase the price of the insurance or might make the house uninsurable.

2.9 TITLE SEARCH

This clause gives a title search company the time to do a title search, which will begin when the property was first built and continue on until the present owner. The title company is looking for unpaid liens or taxes or any contested ownership like a divorce decree or the terms of someone's will. People have lost houses because someone was able to produce a valid will from a hundred years ago stating that the property was rightfully inherited by their ancestor and not by the person who took possession of the property.

2.10 VACATING THE SELLER

You can determine the time to seller has to vacate the premises. You might want to take possession quickly, say in thirty days. Or you might already have a few projects going and are willing to give the seller a longer time period to move out.

2.11 TERMITE INSPECTION

This is separate from the home inspection and is a requirement in many states before the lender will hand over the money. Termite damage can be used to negotiate a lower price, and an active infestation will need to be addressed before the lender will close the deal.

2.12 LEAD PAINT OR ASBESTOS INSPECTION

This is probably more common in large cities where you are dealing with houses that are over one hundred years old. Removing lead paint or asbestos is an expensive proposition and you certainly can't rent to anyone if lead paint or asbestos is present on the property.

2.13 MOLD INSPECTION

This will tell you if there is mold present on the property. Mold can also be quite expensive to remove.

2.14 PRIVATE WELL INSPECTION

In more rural areas where there is no city water piped in and people rely on well water, it is necessary to test the well to make sure the water is potable (fit for human consumption).

2.15 HOA RULES

This will give you time to inspect the rules of the Home Owner's Association (HOA) and decide if you want to purchase the property. Some HOA rules are as strict as how long your garage door can be left open, where your garbage can should be located, and whether or not you can put lawn furniture or ornaments in the front yard. Remember that your tenant will also need to follow these rules. Some people refuse to buy a property for rental use if the neighborhood has an HOA and some people will not rent there.

All of the possible contingencies do not need to be used, or you can even write an offer with no contingencies. Some, like the home inspection, are there to protect your interest. Some, like the appraisal, are mandatory and will be done anyway so it is a good idea to have something in writing that puts you in control of the situation. And contingencies can be used as a bargaining tool. If a house does not appraise for what the seller is asking you can ask them to lower the price. If the home inspection states that the house needs a new roof you can ask the seller to lower the price enough to cover the cost, you will need to put out for the new roof.

So the offer has gone to the seller and they have accepted your offer. All of the contingencies, if any, have been met. The seller may also be required by law to provide certain documents such as that earthquake zone or floodplain designations. The seller is also required to disclose any defects they already know about the property. Usually these are disclosed before now but in the event, they are kept secret until this point, or something new has happened, this is your last chance to walk away from the purchase. If you make the decision to go ahead with the purchase you will give your agent a small amount of non-refundable money, called earnest money, which shows that you are serious about buying this property.

Between the time that all parties agree to the deal and the day the papers are actually signed there is a lot going on. This is the time when the inspections and appraisal are done, the title search is completed, and the lender is gathering all the documents it needs to prove your worthiness to receive their money. The attorneys are looking over documents for any flaws. During this time, you may want to do a final walk through of the property, especially if it is vacant, to make sure no other repair issues have come up and to make sure the seller did not remove anything that was supposed to stay. If you are doing a full rehab, you might not care if the light fixtures are missing but if the house was in good condition and ready to rent those missing light fixtures will cost you money. Situations like these are easier to address before the sale is final.

On the appointed day at the appointed time all parties will meet at the closing. You will be there with your agent, the seller will be there with their agent, and the attorney and a secretary or paralegal will be present. You will sign more papers than you ever thought it was possible to sign in one sitting. Every piece of paper has a purpose. Every paper will be explained to you before you sign it and you will have the opportunity to read it if you like. Most of these are written in legal jargon, or legalese, and may be difficult for you to understand. This is why you need to have an attorney that you trust look over the papers before the closing. You will also need to bring your picture identification and any money that you will need to present for closing costs in the form of an official check, or the funds can be wired into an account. You will receive a closing checklist a few days before closing to outline exactly what you will need to bring.

This process is complete and will receive the keys to the property after all of the papers have been signed and you receive a copy of the paperwork and then everyone leaves the office. The paperwork will be filed with the appropriate state office and you are now the legal owner of that property.

The first time you purchase a property it will seem overwhelming and, at times, frustrating. Legal matters move either very slowly or very quickly. Deals may not always go smoothly. Sometimes problems will crop up with the inspections or other contingencies. Trust your agent or your attorney, whoever you are working with, to guide you in the right direction. Later in your career you might consider becoming an agent yourself and bypass some of the steps, but for now trust the experts to guide you.

And you have just purchased your first property.

CHAPTER

THREE

3. TYPE OF PROPERTY TO PURCHASE

One thing that makes investing in real property is the fact that there are so many choices to choose from. These choices offer everyone the opportunity to become an investor in the real estate market is one form or another. But because there are so many choices it is even more important to know exactly which market you want to invest in. You will need to know the details of each type in order to make an informed decision.

Real estate refers to the buildings, land, property, the underground rights below the land, and the air rights directly above the property. The best thing about investing in real estate is that real estate tends to increase in value over the span of years, even if it might have times when the value falls for a few months; it will always regain its worth. The four types of real estate that people might invest in are land, commercial real estate, industrial real estate, and residential real estate.

Industrial real estate is all of the buildings and the land that is suited for or used for activities that are deemed to be industrial in nature. This will include distribution, light storage, research, warehousing, assemble, manufacturing, and production. Have you ever wondered why new warehouses are built in the middle of nowhere? This is because the land out there is inexpensive and that is an asset for an industrial property because they must cover so much space in order to be used as an industrial space.

If the money is right industrial property might be the best market to invest in. Industrial properties are, on the whole, less expensive overall to operate and to own. This gives an investor the ability to own and keep up larger assets that will have a lower capital cost. Industrial real estate also has a more predictable and a more stable cash flow because the leases are much longer than they are in residential property. Industrial leases usually run for several years. Because of this, there will not be many open deals in the industrial real estate market. There are things you will need to consider before you buy a property.

Real estate used for industrial purchases will be found in many sizes and shapes. Industrial real estate will allow quite a bit of flexibility for the needs of the tenant, as long as zoning ordinances are followed. The investor has the freedom to create a new space to suit a new tenant. A building can be a baking facility, technology space, a warehouse for distribution with a small office space, or even a warehouse with no formal office space. The design of the building will definitely determine the kind of tenant you will be able to attract. And for an industrial property you will need to ensure that there is a labor market nearby. An industrial real estate property might be a better investment if it is near a large city with access to public transportation. And be sure to study the market to see what local vacancy rates are. Larger cities that can attract multinational businesses will have a lower vacancy rate than other places will because there are more possible tenants to choose from.

Commercial real estate properties can offer greater financial rewards than residential properties will but they also can have more risk factors than residential real estate. Commercial property refers to mixed use buildings, apartment buildings, industrial buildings, warehouses, office buildings, and retail buildings. There are factors to consider when purchasing each of these types of properties.

Commercial real estate usually has abettor income potential that residential property. Commercial properties annual return on investment is usually between six percent and twelve percent, depending on the area it is located in. Commercial properties can mean less work for the owner, depending on the type of business located there. Since businesses may often work daytime hours there should be few to no overnight calls for a break in or to let in a tenant who has lost their key. Even if the business is a twenty-four-hour operation, it usually has some type of security system or even a security guard that looks over the property.

If the business is a retail operation, it may be easier to manage because retail businesses live by their public image. They will need to look nice in order to draw customers in; therefore, they are more likely to maintain the property which is beneficial for you, the owner. This also creates a better relationship between the property owner and the tenant. And with commercial properties there are usually many tenants that help ease the costs when a unit is empty or a tenant just does not pay their rent.

Buying land is not something that is usually considered when buying real estate for rental property because there is no actual rental property located on it. If you find a piece of land with a quick potential for building residential property, it might be an option but land itself has no option for rental property as long as it is empty.

Residential real estate includes any real estate that people will live in and this includes rental property. Single family homes are the most common of the rental properties but there are also quadplexes, duplexes, triplexes, townhouses, apartment buildings, and condominiums. Apartments and condos are actually considered commercial real estate in most circles but, since they are used for residential properties, they are included in the category of residential rental property.

A single-family dwelling is the property newest real estate investors look at when they are looking for their first properties to purchase. It is the epitome of the American dream; a house for the family to live in. And even though they are not buying it and it is not their own, the majority of tenants will treat a rental property decently since they have to live there. A single-family home is a building that is used and maintained as a single dwelling unit. It will have no common walls with any other residential property. It is built on its own piece of land and does not share land with another property. The single-family home will always have its own private entrance and exit and its own utilities. It was meant to be occupied by one family.

A duplex is a structure that has two separate units, one for each family to occupy. A triplex has three units, and a quadplex has four units. These can be built two, three, or four units in a row as a single- or two-story building, or it can be a large house that was divided into separate apartments. The major difference between a duplex and a townhouse is that the owner of the townhouse also owns the land that his part of the townhouse sits on, where the land in a duplex is owned by one side or the other. This will not matter to you since you will be the owner.

An apartment is a collection of single units in the same building. They are used as rental units and are owned as a whole by one entity, whether that entity is a single person or a management company. A condo, or condominium, is like an apartment in many ways in that there are many condos in one building. The major difference is that an apartment is rented and a condo is owned by the person who lives there. Since most people think of an apartment building as being part of a large complex, the major difference means that, while both units can be rental units, someone who rents a condo usually deals directly with the owner of the unit and someone who rents an apartment deals with the property manager.

This is not to say that a condo is not a good investment for a rental property. Condos have many benefits as rental property units. Condos generally have amenities that apartment owners do not provide unless the apartment is in a high dollar complex. Condos offer a concierge service, fitness center, outdoor areas, garage parking, hot tubs, and swimming pools. This will make owning a condo as a rental unit a more attractive proposition because it should be relatively easy to rent.

An apartment does not need to be a huge complex to be considered an apartment for rental purposes. Apartments can come in many different configurations. Particularly in large cities old houses have been converted into several apartments. If you buy the building, then you own all of the apartments.

But the single family detached home is probably still going to make up the bulk of your inventory for rental properties. Oftentimes investing in single family rental properties is a more appealing opportunity for investment that a multifamily property. If you take the time to carefully invest in the right neighborhoods and markets, a single-family dwelling will often give you a better return on your investment than a multifamily property will. Traditionally single-family units have a lower rate of turnover than multi family or apartment units do. They also offer the following benefits:

3.1 THEY ARE EASIER TO RESELL

You may not want to own a particular piece of property forever. A single-family unit can appeal to a larger market for resale that a multi-family unit would. Since they appeal to both owner-occupiers and investors, they can be easier to sell.

3.2 THEY HAVE LOWER OPERATING COSTS

Usually tenants in a single-family dwelling will pay for all of their own utilities. This will result in a huge savings to you, the owner. And even if you own several single-family units their costs for expenses is usually lower since not all units will need a new roof or new floors at the exact same time.

3.3 YOU HAVE GREATER FLEXIBILITY OVER YOUR PORTFOLIO GROWTH

If you purchase a multifamily unit you have to purchase the entire building at once. This can be a huge monetary investment. But in purchasing single family units, you can buy them one at a time and watch your portfolio grow larger over time. You will also have the flexibility to sell off units that may no longer be profitable.

Especially since you are a new investor in the real estate market, buying single family homes for rental property is the best option to make money with real estate. They require less time and effort than any other kind of rental investment property. And since the price is lower per unit you will get more for your available money. Pretend you have five hundred thousand to spend on a rental investment property. You could probably purchase one commercial property or maybe even two multifamily units at two hundred fifty thousand each. But if you find five houses to buy for rental properties and all together they cost five hundred thousand dollars, then you have just purchased five properties instead of one or two.

Financial institutions like to lend money on single family homes. They see these purchases as low-risk investments. Single family homes keep their stability in the real estate market, even if the market is fluctuating. They tend to hold their value longer. An investor can usually get a lower down payment, a lower rate of interest on the loan and sometimes even higher loan-to-value ratios when they are financing single family homes.

The rental income produced does not determine the value of a single-family home. The value of a single-family dwelling can often be improved with a few minor cosmetic repairs. Other types of investment rental property are more difficult to raise the value on because it involves locating new tenants or even adding more units to the whole, which would involve a major construction project. And single-family homes appreciate or increase in value, faster than other types of rental property. Again, this is because the value is tied to factors other than simply the rental income. The single-family dwelling is also valued on its décor, amenities, and location; and if there is less supply than there is demand for then the value will increase.

Managing a single-family home is probably the easiest management job you will ever do. Part of this is due to the fact that turnover is much lower. If you are able to locate good tenants as renters, they will stay longer. There are many reasons for this fact. Sometimes a family is saving to buy their own house so they stay in one place to avoid constantly paying moving costs. Tenants usually leave apartments to move into single family dwellings. Sometimes good tenants will begin to think of their rental unit as their own property and will take care of it that way. Some people will never have the cash available to own their own home, either for the down payment or the monthly upkeep, but they can manage to pay a monthly rental payment. And some people have absolutely no desire to ever own their own home. All of these factors make people good tenants and make your job of finding and keeping tenants much easier.

When choosing a single-family house to purchase as a rental property, there are things that you must consider before you start laying out money for the purchase.

3.4 AVERAGE LOCAL RENTS

Since you will be making your money from the rental income, you will need to know what the average rent in the area is. And whatever you decide to charge for rent will need to cover your expenses for the property, taxes, insurance, and mortgage payment.

3.5 NATURAL DISASTERS

Since the homeowner's insurance is one of the expenses the rent will need to cover, you will need to know up front how much insurance you will need and what it will cost. Houses located in areas that flood or have earthquakes might not support the rent needed to cover the extra insurance.

3.6 LOCAL VACANCIES AND LISTINGS

If there are a number of listings or vacancies it might be a seasonal thing or it might mean that the area is in decline. Since most people move in the summer months to get settled before the next school year a quantity of listings in June is not a bothersome as the same quantity of listings in October. And an area with a high rate of vacancies will not support the rent you might need to make positive cash flow.

3.7 POSSIBLE FUTURE DEVELOPMENT

Any new growth and development in the area will be the responsibility of the local planning and development office so be sure to check with them before purchasing a rental dwelling. Future rezoning could help or hurt your investment. Future planned development of a shopping center nearby will benefit your investment, where the development of a recycling center would probably hurt your chances of renting your investment to a tenant.

3.8 LOCAL AMENITIES

Drive around the neighborhood and look for public libraries, parks, public transportation, movie theaters, gyms, and restaurants. All of these are amenities that people like to have near either where they work or where they live.

3.9 LOCAL HABITS

Also take a drive through the neighborhood on different days and at different times of the day and night. A neighborhood that is quiet and peaceful on Sunday afternoon just might turn into a block party on Saturday night. Your new tenant might not like that so you need to know these things up front before you buy.

3.10 LOCAL JOB MARKET

Tenants will be more attracted to areas that have job availability if needed. The local government can give you statistics on job availability for a particular area. And definitely check and see if any new businesses are opening up in the areas because new businesses require new employees and those employees need somewhere to live.

3.11 CRIME RATES

Check the frequency of criminal activity in the area where you plan to buy a rental property. Look at the rates for petty crimes as well as serious crimes and the rates for burglary and vandalism. No one wants to move into a high crime area and that perfect rental property might be less than perfect if it is in an area prone to crime.

3.12 SCHOOLS

Buying a home large enough for a family will mean that the area needs to support good schools. Buying a house in an area where there are substandard schools or no schools will seriously affect your ability to rent and will also affect its resale value in the future.

3.13 ASSESSED PROPERTY TAXES

The location of the house will affect the amount of property tax you will be required to pay. The taxes will need to be paid out of the money you are paid for the monthly rent. A great neighborhood with classier homes will support the higher property taxes required but there are plenty of downtrodden neighborhoods that have high property taxes. It is also a good idea to check the financial stability of the town or city because future property tax hikes used to cover government costs can price you right out of the market.

3.14 NEIGHBORHOOD

This is probably the most important consideration. The neighborhood will be a determining factor in lowering your vacancy rates and attracting good tenants. It might be easy to find tenants for a house near a college in August but will the house still be occupied the next July? A neighborhood near a highway might be attractive to renters who commute to downtown for work every day but not so attractive to a young couple with children. It is best to try to find the most desirable neighborhoods even if this limits your home choices a bit. You can always make upgrades to the house but you cannot change the neighborhood.

Like many rental property investors have learned before you, the single-family home in the right neighborhood is the best opportunity for good rental property. These properties are easy to purchase and equally easy to sell if needed. You will not need to put a lot of effort into property management with good tenants. You will not need to deal with high expenses. The choice is simple—go for the single-family dwelling.

CHAPTER
FOUR

4. CREATE AND BUILD YOUR TEAM

S o your plan is to start with one rental property and build an impressive portfolio of different rental properties in different parts of town all designed to provide you with the type of cash flow that will definitely give you the money you need to build savings for an early retirement. Well, you have your plan in place. Now, you need to build your team. Planning for your future means having a competent team of people ready to do what you need to help you grow the way you want to grow. Don't worry; you do not need to add all of these people at the same time but sooner rather than later is best. And keep in mind when it is referred to the person joining your team that does not necessarily mean the person works just for you. Most of these people will have their own businesses and will also work for other people. But when you need that particular skill, they will be the person you will go to.

The first person to join your team will likely be your real estate agent. You can most likely locate available properties on your own. Your first few properties might even be located this way. But what about when you have many properties to take care of? And just exactly how do you find a house to buy and how do you do the paperwork required. You need a good real estate agent. And while the agent works for many people when they work for you, they know exactly what you are looking for. They can find you the best rental properties for your investment purposes. They might even come across a property when you aren't actively looking for a new property. Their job is to take the wants and needs you give them and find the right property for you. Then, they will take care of all the paperwork related to the purchase of the home. Of course, you will need to pay for all of this expertise, usually six percent of the sale price of the house but do you really want to take the risk of doing something wrong with the closing paperwork?

Your real estate agent is the professional who makes their money by matching people and properties. They don't make any money if they don't do their job so it is in their best interests to find you properties to buy. And they have the ability to filter searches by location, local amenities, size, and configuration of the house you desire. They can also provide you with facts and figures about the property that you will need to know in order to decide if this property will be profitable for you.

Your agent will also be beneficial when you go to tour the house. They can often point out where improvements to the property might be made and different uses for rooms inside the home—this room could be a bedroom, a den, or an office. They will not just walk through the house with you or leave you to walk through alone. They will figuratively hold your hand and lead you along.

The next professional you need to add to your team is the real estate attorney. People do not always think of hiring an attorney to buy a house yet it has contracts and searches that an attorney might be the best person to handle. Their first major task they will handle for you is to review all of the contracts involved in purchasing a house to make sure you are getting the best possible deal. Real estate contracts are filled with legal words and real estate uses legal terms that are peculiar to real estate. It is almost mandatory to have a good real estate attorney on your side.

Straight seller to buyer transactions are not the only real estate transactions you will likely make and this is where a real estate attorney will be a valuable asset. You might come across a wonderful property that is part of an estate sale, a sale from a partnership or trust, or even a sale from a lending institution or a corporation. The more people involved and the more steps involved the more important it is to have a good real estate attorney on your side. And between the purchase agreement and the final closing is the title search. The title search is your guarantee that the person selling you the home is the sole legal owner of the home and they have the right to sell it to you. Sometimes a negative issue is discovered, such as an old unpaid lien or tax bill. An attorney can provide solutions for taking care of these little annoyances so that the sale of the house can proceed and provide the proof that they have been satisfied.

Your insurance agent is right up there in importance with your real estate agent and your real estate attorney. You do not want to purchase a property that you do not insure. First, you are required to carry insurance on a property that has a mortgage attached to it. This is because the lender wants their money in the event that the property is damaged and not fit for human habitation. Second, if you pay cash for the house you will want to protect and ensure your investment. Without adequate insurance, you will be out all that money if something happens to the house.

Anyone can purchase insurance online and probably get a really good policy to protect their interests. But working with an actual agent will bring you benefits that you can't get shopping online. Insurance is a complicated business. A local agent is someone who lives and works near you and knows the local community. They are there for you not just when you bring them money but also when there is a crisis and you need your agent.

The premiums you pay for your homeowner's insurance will depend on the amount of coverage that you need. Of course, the minimum the house will be insured for is the amount required to pay off the mortgage if the house burns down. But you will likely want coverage that will replace the house if it is a total loss. They will know if your particular rental property has a value higher than the homes around it, thus causing it to need extra coverage.

A local agent will know the area. They will be able to address the need for extra insurance to cover possible natural disasters. They will know which areas of town are prone to localized issues such as sewer backups or flooding problems during heavy rains. He will know how to insure each property you own to get the best possible coverage for that house for the best possible price.

And since he sees you and knows you, he will keep your best interests close to his heart. He will call you if a payment is late. He will look for ways to save you money on your policies. And he will monitor the local markets looking for increases in home values that might require an increase in your policy limits.

You will need an accountant one day. Maybe not with your first property but as your portfolio grows you will find that juggling all the tax related facts and figures will likely be a full-time job. Hire an accountant when the figures become too confusing to wade through. Yes, you will need to pay them but the amount you pay them is minuscule compared to the amount you could lose by not keeping proper records and doing your taxes the right way.

An accountant will help you to structure your investments and operations in a manner that will make you tax efficient. Your accountant will help you with tax reporting activities as well as planning your investments and preparing your budgets. They will keep track of all your financial records and prepare any financial report you might need.

Your accountant can prepare reports detailing your profits and expenses, developmental expenses, and operational costs. They will keep tabs on your lease agreement payments, cash-based income statements, revenues, and expenditures. And by having access to all of your financial reports they will be able to recommend other financial and investment opportunities that will help you grow your personal wealth. They can also help you with suggestions for creative financing for future purchases.

When you have one property or even several properties you can probably manage them on your own. This means being available to do repairs at all hours of the day or night and to be on call if there is an emergency at the rental property, like a fire or a tree crashed into the living room. Maybe you don't want to deal with these issues. This is when you need a property manager. Most people will find that hiring a property management company gives them the most freedom to continue building their business while ensuring their existing properties are well taken care of.

The property management company will assist you in setting rental rates. They will have access to reports that list local market rates and will help you come up with a price that will meet your cash flow needs while not pricing you out of the market. They will collect the monthly rents from the tenants for you and they will deposit those rents in the proper account. They will be responsible for advertising and marketing your property. They will know exactly where and how to market your property to find the best mix of possible tenants for you.

They will screen possible tenants and find the right fit for your property according to your specifications. They will run security checks and background checks on potential tenants. They will also collect previous landlord references, employment verification, and credit reports. And in addition to finding the right tenant for your property, they will manage those tenants for you by providing both emergency and routine maintenance, manage conflict resolutions, and take care of any routine inspections that might be needed.

And the property management company will keep up to date on all applicable landlord tenant laws and will alert when something might affect your particular properties. A good property manager will help you avoid possible legal issues by keeping you informed of changes in the law and keeping your property legally compliant. And perhaps most importantly of all, having a property manager will allow you the freedom to keep growing your portfolio and to enjoy your life.

The day will come when you will need to hire someone to make needed repairs at one of your properties. Whether you hire a general handyman or a licensed contractor is dependent on the job that needs to be done and personal desires. But when something happens in one of your properties that require immediate attention, you might not possess the tools, skills, or time to fix it yourself. This is when you will need to hire someone who can fix the broken thing for you.

A general handyman is a person who probably is not licensed but has experience fixing things in and around houses. They keep their own equipment and tools. Since they do not need to be licensed there may be a large amount of variability in the quality of the work provided from one handyman to another. If you are using a handyman type of person make sure you get references from other people, at the very least. It might be a good idea to make sure they are bonded and insured. Having their own insurance will cover them if they are injured while working on your property. Being bonded means that a bonding company is holding money to pay a consumer in case they need to file a claim against the individual or the company, in the event that they handyman steals something from your property or damages it somehow.

A contractor may work for a company or be an independent. They are a licensed professional who has gone through a certain amount of training in a specific area or areas. Contractors are bonded and insured and they will be responsible for hiring sub-contractors who will actually do some of the work that they may not be able to do or while they are doing other work.

Hiring a professional contractor can be quite expensive. Hiring a handyman is generally done by the hour or the job. A contractor might not be available for as many hours as a handyman might be willing to work for. And while a contractor is trained to do certain job that does not mean that the handyman can't do the same jobs equally well.

It might be a good idea and there is certainly nothing wrong with the idea of hiring both a handyman and a general contractor. Since a contractor usually either works for a contracting company or owns his own company, he will have other work available besides yours. You would definitely hire a contractor for large renovations or large property repairs. But a handyman can easily handle small projects and minor property repairs and may respond quicker than the contractor.

These are the people you will want on your team to help you grow your real estate rental property portfolio and to make the biggest return on investment that you could possible make. However, you bring them together you will be the one who will need to decide how soon you need them and if they are the person who will help you grow your business. Planning for your future requires investments of time as well as money and a good team will be able to save you both.

CHAPTER
FIVE

5. DEALS, FINANCING, AND NO MONEY DOWN

When people traditionally purchase a house they want to make their home, they will diligently save the down payment amount and then secure a mortgage to cover the remaining amount. But that is no longer the only method for buying a house. If this was still the only way available, very few people would be buying rental property or houses in general. Creative thinking will get your business off the ground.

One way to finance your new purchase is to get the seller to finance the loan for you. This means that instead of getting a traditional loan you will make your mortgage payments to the original owner. This will result in much less paperwork than a traditional loan if you find a seller who is willing to do it. This scenario can work a number of different ways. The seller might be the owner looking to downsize from a property he has long since paid off. The seller might also be a property investor with more ready funds than you have built up. The seller might finance the entire price of the purchase or only just the down payment. This method will only be successful for both parties if they agree on what is a fair rate of interest for this loan. Before you gain enough knowledge and experience it is wise to check with your attorney and/or your accountant. And always get both parties to agree to the terms of the loan in writing.

It is well worth saying again—Get the Terms in Writing! Get everything in writing, with signatures attached. The times of conducting business with a handshake are long gone and you need to have written proof of everything in order to survive in today's business world. If someone refuses to put their words and terms in writing and add their signature, think about this—do you really want to do business with that person? Get it in writing and cover your own assets.

If you can find another person that you trust completely, you might find a very profitable venture in a partnership. You will need to find a partner who has liquid money ready to be able to make the down payment. This strategy is particularly effective if you know someone who would like to get involved in real estate but does not want to do the daily work of finding properties, collecting rental payments, and looking for new tenants. This person is known as a silent partner—someone who provides needed funds but does not want to have an equal share or say in how the business is run.

So in this example, one person brings the money and the other person—you—brings the work. The key to success here is in agreeing how to split the proceeds from the rental property. One way to do this is for the silent partner to be repaid, plus interest, in a set amount of time. If the silent partner is getting more of the proceeds from the house, then you would need to decide with them exactly how to divide the proceeds between you two. It might come out as a nearly equal split because, while your partner is providing all the money needed, you are providing all the daily work needed. You will need to devise a split that will be fair to both parties.

Again, get the deal in writing. This is needed to save both of you because giving someone a chunk of money can be a risky proposition and you don't want to later be held to terms that were never agreed on in the first place. So go to your attorney and draw up a mutually agreeable contract between the two of you. The attorney might also think of things that your partners never thought of. This document is called an operating agreement and it is just that—an agreement that tells you both how this deal will operate.

There are in place today programs run by the government that will help people buy houses. In fact, the Federal Housing Administration (FHA) was originally put into place to encourage people to purchase houses. One of the methods it uses successfully is to give people the opportunity to buy houses with a very low-down payment. FHA loans are designed specifically to enable people to buy homes they will occupy but it is allowable to buy a multifamily unit such as a duplex or a triplex and for the owner to rent all but one unit which he keeps for himself. You don't need to live there forever and this is a wonderfully cost-effective method for financing rental properties, especially if it is the first property you are purchasing.

You can also borrow from your retirement account. If you have worked long enough to build up any amount of money in a retirement account, then you can use it. This method allows you to borrow from yourself and repay yourself over time with interest. It is a win-win situation because it provides the ready cash for the down payment while giving your retirement fund a little boost. Again, consult with your accountant or your attorney to make certain the risk is worth the reward.

Anyone who is applying for an FHA loan might want to consider having a cosigner or a co-borrower to help them apply for the loan. Having one of these might improve your chances of success in actually getting the loan. Using another person is also a good way to for a borrower who hasn't yet established credit or who has less than perfect credit to be able to purchase a rental property.

A co-signer and a co-borrower are not the same thing. Co-borrowers have more benefits than a co-signer does even though the amount of responsibility that they share is relatively equal. A co-borrower is obligated to pay the mortgage and has the same right to possession that the other borrower does. The co-borrower's credit history, liabilities, assets, and income will all be considered as part of their credit worthiness just like yours will be. The co-signer must also present proof of credit worthiness with their credit history, assets, liabilities, and income but they do not have any legal interest in the ownership of the property. They will, however, be responsible for repaying the loan in the event that the other person can't. The problem with this method is in finding someone who is willing to take a risk on your business venture.

If you are already purchasing a home, you might be able to get a second mortgage on your home to use for down payment money on a rental property purchase. A second mortgage is just another type of mortgage loan that will allow you to borrow an amount of money that is based on the value of your home to use for other purposes. The money you are borrowing against is the equity in your home. The equity of your home is the difference between the fair market value of your home and the amount that you still owe on your mortgage. Fair market value is the value that has been assigned to your home that someone would offer for it if it was for sale, not the monetary value you might ask for if you were selling it.

A second mortgage can be paid to you in one of several different ways. The traditional method is a lump sum payment where the lender will give you a check for a predetermined amount and you will pay it back monthly just like you pay your current mortgage payment. The term of repayment for a second mortgage is generally much less than the time allowed for a first mortgage because the amount is usually much smaller than the original mortgage amount. The other way to get a second mortgage is to take out a HELOC, a home equity line of credit. With this type of loan, the lender sets a maximum allowed borrowing limit and the money is held in reserve for when you want to use it. Then you take funds out as needed and repay any funds that you have used in regular monthly payments. Unlike a lump sum payment, the payment amount for a HELOC will vary each month according to what you have borrowed. You are under no obligation to use any or the entire amount. You can access the money by going to the lender and getting an official check, a transfer to a checking account or a wire transfer to another account. You pay a HELOC back much like you repay a credit card you have used.

Second mortgages have advantages and disadvantages. One big advantage is that you can get one when the interest rates are low and get a fixed rate of interest. This will help keep your payments lower over the life of the loan. A second mortgage can give you the opportunity to borrow an amount much larger than a personal line would. And since it is a mortgage loan the interest part of the monthly repayment might be tax deductible (again, consult your accountant). One of the disadvantages to a second mortgage is that they are treated like a first mortgage and have nearly the same amount of paperwork involved with the same closing costs, credit analysis, origination fees, appraisals, and much more. And if you are unable to make the payment, or chose not to, you can lose your home because the lender has the same rights as the first mortgage holder to repossess your home and attempt to sell it at auction to recoup their losses. But if done correctly a second mortgage can be a marvelous way to get the down payment you need to have to put down on a rental property without needing to rely on other people.

If you possess one or more credit cards with a higher than average maximum limit then you may be able to get a cash advance that you can use to fund the down payment on a rental property purchase. Just be careful not to exceed your maximum debt to income ratio because this could prevent you from getting a loan for a house. And it is best, if you are using this method, to get the money out in advance of applying for the mortgage loan so that the amount owed is already in place and will appear on your credit report when it is run. Whether you do it before or after you apply for the loan you will still need to explain a large one-time withdrawal like that since your credit report will be run once again just before closing but by doing it before you apply for the mortgage it looks more up front.

And that brings up another good point to make. Your credit report will be pulled (run) when you apply for the mortgage and again a few days before closing. Do not make any large purchases between the two reports. People have been denied a mortgage loan at the last minute because they went out and bought new furnishing for their new house on credit and totally blew up their debt to income ration. This ratio is a formula that lenders use to tell you how much of your income is being eaten up by debt. And just like your mortgage can only be a certain percentage of your income, your debts as a whole are assigned a certain percentage. Exceed that and you may not get your loan.

A hard money loan is a particular kind of loan financing based on assets where a borrower receives funds secured by real property. These loans generally come from investors or private companies. These loans are for projects that will last for a few months to a few years, usually the cost of rehabilitating the property. The rates of interest that are charged on these loans are much higher than it is on regular loans because of the shorter loan period and the higher risk of loss to the investor. The amount a borrower can get is based on the loan to value ratio, which is the total amount of the loan divided by the value of the property. The lender is most concerned with the loan to value ratio when they are lending money for a hard money loan. Lenders will lend this type of loans in two ways. One way is to require a ten to fifteen percent down payment and then the lender will finance one hundred percent of the sale price and rehab costs. If the lender does not require a down payment, they will usually only loan up to seventy percent of the value after the house is repaired (ARV). The ARV is the value of the home after it is fully repaired. So if the ARV of a house is two hundred thousand dollars and it will need twenty-five thousand dollars in repairs, the seventy percent rule states that the lender will finance up to one hundred fifteen thousand dollars. The hard money loan is usually used by people who flip houses for a living.

All cash means just that—all cash. It means that you will pay for the house with cash, no loan. It does not need to be your cash so you can get a gift from someone else. But keep in mind if you enter into a purchase contract and the money disappears then you could be sued. Also, an all cash offer will tie up a good chunk of cash in this house. This type of purchase is also usually used by house flippers.

A conventional loan is any loan from a lender that is not guaranteed or insured by the federal government as VA or FHA loans are. A conventional loan is guaranteed by private lenders and the insurance for it is usually paid by the person borrowing the money. The private lenders are not necessarily private investors by they are banks and credit unions. Loans backed by the government are VA loans, which are only available to military personnel and former military personnel, and FHA loans.

When you get an FHA loan you will be required to make a down payment of a certain percentage, usually three to four percent, and you will be required to pay a mortgage insurance premium which is just an insurance premium that guarantees the loan will be paid. If you default on your loan, the FHA will use part of the mortgage insurance money to repay the loan. You must be active or former military to qualify for a VA loan since these loans are administered by the Veteran's Administration. Getting a loan from the VA does not require a down payment but the borrower will be required to pay a one-time funding fee that is one to three percent of the loan.

When you borrow money from a conventional loan the lender is the one who will lose if you do not pay the loan back (default). If it comes to the point that you can no longer make your loan payments, then the lender will repossess the house and try to sell it quickly to get back as much money as possible. Because of this risk factor, most conventional loan borrowers will be required to pay mortgage insurance from a private source (PMI) if you have a down payment of less than twenty percent of the purchase price.

Loans are usually fixed rate loans with a set payment every month. This means that the monthly payment will be the same every month whether it is the first payment or the last payment. Sometimes loans are written as adjustable rate mortgage loans (ARM) which mean that periodically the interest rate will not remain the same but will raise or fall depending on the prime rate, which is a rate that large banks set and is the rate at which they loan money to other banks. ARMs are attractive if your income increases periodically like the mortgage payment might, but if your income does not keep up with the increases in the mortgage rate then you may not be able to make your monthly payments. Sometimes, people will start the loan as an ARM and refinance to a conventional loan before the mortgage adjusts for the first time.

Two things to steer clear from at all costs are balloon payments and prepayment penalties. A balloon payment is assessed at the end of an interest only loan. If you are paying off an interest only loan then you will only pay the interest for the life of the loan and then the entire principle, the amount you borrowed, is due on demand from the bank. It will either need to be paid or financing acquired for it. A prepayment penalty is a penalty assessed by the lending agency if you pay the loan off early. Neither of these is used very often but they can be so watch for them.

You may want to look at different options for financing your purchases based on how many properties you own. Whichever financing avenue you choose, just make sure to consult with your attorney or your accountant to insure that you will be getting the best deal possible.

CHAPTER

SIX

6. TO FLIP OR NOT TO FLIP

Flipping a house is basically the process of buying a house and fixing it up and intending to sell it for a profit. It can also be used successfully by people who want to get into the real estate rents property game. Usually, houses that need to be fixed up will sell at a lower price than a house that is cosmetically perfect so these houses can be easier to purchase because of the lower price.

House flipping is about as basic as you can get in the world of real estate investing. To be a successful flipper you will want to buy at a low price, fix it up at a reasonable price, and sell it at a high price. The goal is to find a house that is priced less than it is worth or needs just enough work to be easy to fix up and sell. Some people have built their entire career and their entire portfolio around flipping houses for profit.

You will need to carefully research the local market before you decide to buy a project house. Every market will not be suitable for your house flipping journey. This is why you should decide on your budget before you buy. If you only have a budget of twenty thousand dollars, you will not be looking at houses that cost seven hundred thousand dollars. When you have less on-hand cash to work with then you will need to be more careful where you purchase. Financing for an investment property will cover the major part of your purchase but there is a big difference between a twenty percent down payment for a fifty-thousand-dollar property and a twenty thousand dollar down payment for a five hundred-thousand-dollar property. So decide how much money you have available to spend and then begin to pick the appropriate market.

One way many real estate investors go about finding the appropriate neighborhood is to classify the possible neighborhoods as A, B, C, and D. Neighborhoods that are in Class A are the wealthiest neighborhoods the housing market offers you. These are the neighborhoods that are inhabited by high-income professional people. Class B neighborhoods are those that are populated by the solid middle-class families. Blue collar neighborhoods are the Class C neighborhoods, filled with working-class people. The bottom of the neighborhood class ladder is the Class D neighborhood which houses the lower income earners. The key for success will be to choose the neighborhood where your money can do the best and where you feel the most comfortable. You might have the financial resources to flip houses in the Class A neighborhood but do you really feel comfortable there? Are you happy looking at high end finishes and planning myriads of one-use rooms for a potential buyer? Or are you more comfortable in the Class C or D neighborhood where you might be doing a real service for good people looking for a house to rent? Either way is just fine but you need to decide which way is best for you before you buy your first property.

Class D neighborhoods might come with their own set of anomalies. They may come with risks not found in the other neighborhood types. Insurance premiums might be higher for these houses because the crime rate might be higher or it might give the impression of being higher. Remember that it is not always the act that drives the cost of insurance but the possibility of the act. A house being flipped in a Class D neighborhood might be more likely to be vandalized or burglarized.

A property that is located in a Class B or C neighborhood might be the best location for your first flip. These are solid middle class and stable working-class neighborhoods that will usually have a lower rate of crime involved. A flipped house that is structurally sound and cosmetically attractive will entice renters to move there relatively easily. When you choose your first house to flip try to look for houses that only require cosmetic updates. Replacing a few fixtures in the bathroom and kitchen, new cabinets, fresh paint and flooring, and a little curb appeal, these will get you the biggest return on your investment and will get you a house suitable for renting in the shortest amount of time.

Eventually you will purchase a more complicated flip or that you are not qualified to do it. But the first house needs to be relatively easy for several reasons. An easier house to flip will cost less money and it will build your confidence. And a house that is ready quickly is one you won't get tired of and one that can be used as leverage in your next real estate deal.

When you have successfully flipped your first few houses then you can look at more complicated flips. But in the beginning, you do not want to deal with structural issues like a cracked or sinking foundation. You also don't want to deal with mechanical issues like replacing the HVAC (heating, ventilation, air conditioning) system or relocating the breaker box for the electrical system. Both of these involve pulling permits, which is getting permission from the local government to do the work. Then someone from the proper governmental agency will come out to inspect the work. This type of flip will come in time; be patient.

You will definitely need to have your financing in place before looking at properties so that when you find a good one you will be ready to make an offer. Because if you find a flip that will be a good deal, then someone else will find it a good deal, too. When you purchase a house that needs rehab work, you don't get a mortgage loan you get a bridge loan. This loan will "bridge" the time between buying the property and selling the property. If you decide to keep the property, which is the main goal of this exercise, then you will replace the bridge loan with a mortgage loan.

This is the time when you will need to hire a contractor or build relationships with several contractors. If it is at all possible, go to sites they are working on so that you are able to see some of their work. It is a good idea to get several bids for rehabbing the property even before you make an offer on the property. If the bids you are getting are way out of line than what you were planning to spend, maybe this is not the house for you. And whatever budget amount you settle on, add twenty percent to that amount. This will cover any unexpected costs that might come up. For example, when pulling out the kitchen cabinets to replace them you might find damage to the wall behind the sink that will need to be fixed. It might be easier to replace the wallboard than to spend the time removing the wallpaper that seems to have been there forever. This extra twenty percent is your contingency fund, in case things happen you weren't expecting.

Flipping houses is a worthless venture if you do not know how to find the house in the first place. And you will want to find a good deal. Your realtor might be able to help you find a house that needs a little loving to be beautiful again. And since you are just starting out it might be a good idea to remain close to home. Since you already live in the neighborhood, then you should already know plenty of information about it.

Finding a flip in your personal geographic region gives you several advantages. As we said, you already know the neighborhood. You will know better than most which parts of town are still popular for people to move into and which parts have lately become more unfavorable. You will understand the attractions of the neighborhood and the local culture. This will mean that you will have a better knowledge of the home's value besides the figures that are on paper.

And living close physically to your project will make it much more convenient for you to get to work and to be able to oversee the project. This alone will save you money and time. If the project is close by then you will be able to see the project regularly if you are not actively working on it during the rehab project. This will give you the opportunity to regularly meet with the contractors and sub-contractors. And you will be nearby to be able to show the home to potential renters, something that your property manager will do for you when you hire them, in addition to overseeing the renovation. By taking care of the first few projects yourself, you will have more of an understanding of the kind of performance you will expect from your manager.

Having limited experience flipping houses may mean you will want to stick to houses that will be assured of renting quickly. This will likely mean that your goal will be the basic three-bedroom, two-bathroom house that will be suitable for most families. It will also not be too big of a house to put your efforts into. A house of this size with minimal renovations should be ready to rent inside of two to three months.

And when you are planning your renovations and looking at prices for material, make sure you prepare a good estimate of the overall cost so that you can set a proper budget. When you pick out what looks like the perfect floor time don't forget to price the glue, grout, baseboard, and any tools that you might need. And if someone else is laying this floor tile you, will need to pay for that person's labor bill.

And when we say stick to easy rehabilitation that means the projects that are the easiest but will bring you the biggest financial return. You might need to replace all the cabinets, appliances, and fixtures in the kitchen and bathrooms but if you keep the existing floor plan and go with what is called builder's grade fixtures, you can do all of this for very little money. Put fresh paint on the walls and lay new flooring. Going with laminate over carpet is the better choice for rental housing because the floors are easier to maintain and won't stain or hold odors like carpet will. Don't overlook things like outlet covers and wall switch covers; replacing all of them is inexpensive but will make the walls look finished. Anything that you are not painting or replacing will need to be scrubbed meticulously, especially the windows. Dirt will not look attractive to a potential renter.

No matter what kind and style of fixtures you choose for this house, the most important piece of advice ever is to maximize the potential of your return by limiting the amount of financial risk you take. This simply means to not pay too much for the house you buy and this requires knowing exactly what the house will be worth when it is finished and the potential cost of the needed repairs. When you have this information, you will then be better able to decide on an ideal purchase price.

Pay close attention to the seventy percent rule. This rule states that you should not pay more than seventy percent of the after-repair value of the house. This is the value of the house after the house is repaired fully. Think of it this way: if the after-repair value of the home is one hundred thousand dollars and the house needs twenty-five thousand dollars' worth of repair work, then according to the seventy percent rule you should not pay more than forty five thousand dollars for the house.

$100,000 x 70% = $70,000 - $25,000 = $45,000

The after-repair value is the value that the house would sell for if you were going to sell it. So, since you are flipping this house to keep and rent to a tenant, then you have just paid forty-five thousand dollars for a house that could potentially be worth one hundred thousand dollars, which is instant equity in your pocket.

Flipping houses is a business venture just like owning real estate for rental property is. Just like being a landlord, flipping houses is the kind of business that will require effort, skill, patience, planning, money, and time. It will most likely end up being more expensive and more difficult than what you ever expected it to be. And even the flippers and landlord who get every detail just right can sometimes fail. This is not a quick scheme for you to get rich but a steady lifelong plan to grow your personal wealth.

CHAPTER
SEVEN

7. FINDING TENANTS

Now you have purchased your first house and have it fully renovated. Now it is time to find a tenant to rent your property and help you begin to build your empire. The only way to have good tenants for your rental properties is to promote your properties in the best way possible. There are three major ways to find new tenants: you can hire a property management firm, you can hire a real estate agent, or you can find them yourself. There are specific methods that each choice offers and each choice has its own particular disadvantages and advantages.

If you prefer to find your tenants yourself then you will be the one who is responsible for finding people to live in your house. You personally will need to market your property answer questions over the phone and by email, take people in to see the property, and choose the best possible tenant from all the people that apply. By using the most methods to advertise your rental property, you will have a larger pool of people who might want to rent it.

It may sound old school but a sign that says "For Rent" will still attract attention from people driving past. This actually still works especially well because some people will be out driving through the neighborhood because they are specifically looking for a house in that neighborhood. You can put the sign in the front yard, in the front window, or on nearby corners with the address written on it. Just make sure you don't put the signs on corners where they are not allowed by local laws.

Advertise your rental property on rental websites and on Craigslist and other sites like it. Using the internet to get the word out that you have a rental property is perhaps the easiest way to do it. Everyone is online nowadays. Most of these websites are free to the landlord so there will be no cost involved for reaching so many people. And if you are a seasoned investor or even if you are just beginning, if you have already put up your own website then this will be your first offering.

In various areas some neighborhoods have formed groups on social media and this would be a great place to list your rental property if there is a social media group for that particular neighborhood. You might be allowed to join the group in order to post your rental there. After all, as the owner of the home you are technically a member of the neighborhood.

Don't overlook print media as a place to advertise your rental property. There are many options for this beyond the local newspaper. Seek out community newsletters and local free press publications. These are generally distributed at restaurants, bars, and coffee shops around town, so they will automatically increase your range of coverage for no cost.

Tell everyone you know that you are the proud owner of a rental property and it is ready for rent. Coworkers, relatives, neighbors, and friends can all help you spread the word. Do not take for granted the person that Uncle Joe sends you will be a good match. Continue with the same screening process for personal referrals that you plan to use for everyone else.

When you are posting your rental property online you will naturally want to post pictures of the outside and the inside. People are more likely to become excited about a property if they have an idea what it will look like before they get there. This allows them the time to begin mentally arranging their furniture before they ever walk in the front door. When you take your pictures, take them during the day when the sun is shining. Natural light always makes things look more attractive. Especially inside pictures, people want to see how much natural light will come into the rental property. If there are any dark areas, then turn on a light to illuminate them. Use a camera that is good quality. Definitely do not have any building materials or trash n the picture and do not allow your reflection to show in any of the pictures. There is nothing really wrong with it but it can look creepy. You need to take at least seven to ten pictures and focus on the important areas of the house like the front, the backyard, the kitchen, the bathroom, and the bedrooms.

Make comments about the size and shapes of the various rooms. Several adult tenants sharing the house might want to know if the bedrooms are of a comparable size. A family might want to know if a bedroom is large enough to put two children in comfortably. Describe the property well enough for the tenants to imagine what it looks like. Tell readers what rooms the house has, especially if it has an extra room that could be an office or another bedroom. Let potential renters know if appliances are included. List what amenities are near to the house such as a grocery store, public pool, or a school. Definitely let prospective tenants know what bills they will need to pay besides rent and the minimum amount of time the lease will be signed for. And now is a good time to let them know if pets and smoking will be allowed.

After you have advertised the property and taken tenants through and found out which ones are really interested, then it is time to choose the perfect tenant for your property. Remember, you can't rent one house to everyone so there can only be one winner and you need to make this choice. No method of screening is foolproof but there are certain factors that will help you have a better chance of picking a great tenant.

First you need to make sure you follow the law when you are screening possible tenants. The Federal Fair Housing Act was made to prevent landlords from discriminating against certain classes of people in any way that is related to housing. You are not allowed to disqualify anyone based on their family status, sex, religion, national origin, color, or race or their disability.

You will want to choose a tenant who has a good history of credit. People who have a good credit history are usually responsible people who will treat your property well and pay rent when it is due. It will cost a small fee to run a credit check on a potential renter and it is allowable to ask the tenant to pay for that. When you check a potential tenant's financial record, you are checking for two things. One thing you will want to look for is a person who makes at least three times what the monthly rent is. Any income less than that and they may have trouble paying the rent from time to time even if they have an overall good payment record. You will want to see copies of at least the last months' worth of check stubs; two to three months is better. You can also call their employer to inquire about monthly earnings, attendance record, and length of employment but be warned most employers will not answer your questions themselves. They will probably direct you to use an automated line that will answer your questions.

And when you run their credit check look for several things. Do they have a habit of paying their bills in a timely manner? Check to see what their debt to income ratio is because even if their income is at least the required three times the monthly rent they may have too many other bills that also need to be paid each month. Let's say the rent in your unit is one thousand dollars each month. Tenant A makes three thousand dollars each month but already has two thousand four hundred dollars in bills they owe each month. This tenant will likely have a difficult time paying the rent every month. Tenant B, on the other hand, only makes two thousand five hundred dollars each month but has no other bills to pay. Tenant B is probably a good candidate even though they do not make the required three times salary to monthly rent. And always look for bankruptcies, civil judgments, or any prior evictions.

A criminal background check is almost mandatory these days. You can no longer assume that everyone is a good person. Information about criminal activity is a matter of public record and can easily be seen at the courthouse. When you run this report, it will give you a list of both minor and serious offenses. All you need to run one is the date of birth and the name of the applicant. People who have a criminal record will probably try to hide it, so this is an important report for you to run. And don't just assume that they are who they say they are. Ask each prospective tenant to bring a photocopy of their driver's license where all the information can be seen and check their license yourself to make sure the license they have matches the copy they gave you.

Never forget to check the prospective tenant's rental history. If at all possible, talk to their former landlords. People love to talk about their tenants because it makes them feel important that you are asking for their opinion and they will probably tell you more than you really need to know but that is okay. You will definitely want to know if they paid their rent-on time, why they moved out, what condition they left the property in, and if they gave a proper thirty-day notice. Also, find out if they did any damage to the rental and if they were able to get along reasonably well with their neighbors. You might come across a first-time renter who has all the right qualifications but no rental history. For these people you can ask them to provide a cosigner to help guarantee the rent will be paid on time and regularly.

You especially want to look at the prospective tenant's employment history and their prior addresses. Look to see if they change jobs often or move often. If they do, then your property might be up for rent again before you are ready to deal with it. And if someone does not have a consistent employment record, they may be looking for a new job—and a new place to live—in a few short months.

Remember that the more people you rent to will be more people in the apartment and more people make more noise and mess. And generally, there are only allowed two people per bedroom, unless local laws are different. Think about every situation separately. If two adults with an infant want to rent a one-bedroom unit that can be acceptable and it might be deemed discrimination if you turn them away. But two adults with a teenager leaves one person without a viable bedroom.

Above all trust your instincts. If there is something about a tenant that just does not seem right, do not be afraid to do more digging into their background until you are satisfied that they are a viable tenant. Asking a prospective tenant why they are moving is just like asking someone why they are leaving their job. Just like people should never bad-mouth a former employer, be careful with someone who bad-mouths a former landlord. Yes, there are always two sides to every story but if you find in conversation that everyone else in their lives is to blame for their problems, they may have been a problem tenant at their last rental.

It is common to ask for the first month's rent and a security deposit before a tenant is allowed to move in. The deposit for security is generally the same amount as one month's rent. Before the tenant is allowed to move in you will want to walk through the property with them with a pre-written checklist where you and the tenant will note anything that does not look perfect. Things break. Maybe a bird flew into the bedroom window and made a tiny crack in it. Mark that flaw down, and then have the tenant initial it with you when the item is repaired. You should have two copies of the checklist, one for you and one for the tenant. You sign theirs and they sign yours. You will keep yours to use when you walk through the unit when they move out.

You won't really know until they have moved in whether or not you have chosen good tenants. Doing all of these steps carefully will give you a better chance of having chosen tenants who will love and appreciate your beautiful new property the same way you do.

CHAPTER

EIGHT

8. TERMS YOU NEED TO KNOW

You will come across many terms in the world of real estate that you need to know. Some of them you might use rarely but you will need to understand their meaning so that you can be fully prepared to navigate this new world of real estate rental property.

ACTUAL EVICTION – This is what happens when a tenant does not pay their rent and you need to make them move out so that you can rent the house to someone who will pay the rent.

ADJUSTABLE RATE MORTGAGE – In this type of mortgage, the rate of interest changes over the life of the mortgage at regular intervals such as every two years, every five years, every seven years, or every ten years. This loan can be risky if the rate suddenly jumps up and the payments are too expensive.

AFFIDAVIT – This is a statement that is written out and signed and sworn to in a legal proceeding.

AGREEMENT OF SALE – This is the agreement where the buyer agrees to buy and the seller agrees to sell and the terms are spelled out for everyone to see.

AMENITIES – The things you find in the neighborhood that make it nicer than a neighborhood without amenities. These can include parks, pools, shopping centers, playgrounds, etc.

AMORTIZATION – This is the process where the payments are made up of principal and interest and are paid off over a set amount of years in regular monthly payments. The loan is usually paid off in fifteen, twenty, or thirty years.

APPRAISAL – This is the figure attached to the home that is what the home is worth. An appraiser will set the value of the house based on the property and the selling price of other homes in the area that are just like yours.

APPRECIATION – This is what it is called when the value of the home increases.

ASSESSED VALUE – This is the value given to the house by the tax assessor's office and it is the value used to set the amount of taxes that you will pay.

ASSESSMENT – This is when the government says the owner of the house will pay a certain amount of taxes.

ASSET – Something that you own that can be sold to make money for you.

BALLOON PAYMENT – This is the large leftover payment at the end of a loan that was not paid off by amortization.

BREACH OF CONTRACT – This is what it is called when someone does not live up the terms of a contract that pertain to them.

BUILDING CODE – These are local laws that will specify the minimum standards of the construction of buildings to ensure that they are safe to be in.

BUSINESS – The plan that you will make that will tell how you plan to grow your business.

BUYER'S AGENT – The agent who is helping the buyer in the transaction is the buyer's agent.

CAPITAL GAIN – This is the profit you earn when you sell an asset.

CAPITAL INVESTMENT – This is the money put into building and growing your business.

CASH FLOW – This is the money that is left after all the bills are paid.

CASH RESERVES – This is the amount of money the buyer has left over after the closing costs and the down payment have been paid.

CASUALTY INSURANCE – This is a kind of insurance policy that will protect the owner of the property from injury or loss that comes from events like a vandalism or a theft.

CAVEAT EMPTOR – This is a Latin phrase that means "let the buyer beware". This just means that the buyer needs to pay attention to what they are buying.

CHATTELS – This is a term that just means personal property.

CLOSING – These will be about two to ten percent of the purchase price of the house and they will be paid when you go for the closing. These fees cover the excise taxes, title insurance, and costs for processing the loan.

COLLATERAL – This is something of value that is promised to a lender to ensure the loan is repaid. The house would be the collateral for the mortgage loan.

COMMERCIAL PROPERTY – This type of real estate includes properties that make money like stores, hotels, shopping centers, office buildings, and restaurants.

COMMISSION – This is the money the real estate agent or realtor gets when they help the seller sell the house.

COMPARABLE – This is the term that means the properties in the neighborhood that have already sold and are very much like your house.

COMPARATIVE MARKET ANALYSIS – This is the report that lists houses in the area that are very like your house and it is used to determine the value of the house.

CONDOMINIUM – This is one unit in a multi-unit building that can be bought and sold like a free-standing house can.

CONTINGENCIES – These are the conditions that will need to be met before the house sale can be finalized.

CONTRACT – A legal agreement that is entered into by two or more parties where someone agrees to do something and receive something in return.

CONVENTIONAL LOAN – A mortgage loan that does not have the guarantee of the government.

COUNTEROFFER – This is the offer that the seller might make in response to the buyer's offer when the seller wants more money or different terms.

CREDIT SCORE – This is a three-digit number that rates the level of credit an individual has. The higher the credit score the better. You get a good credit score by having credit and paying your bills on time.

CUL-DE-SAC – The dead end of a dead-end street where the street gets wide enough for a car to turn around in a circle.

DBA – These initials mean Doing Business As.

DEBT – This is something that you owe to someone else.

DEED – This is the piece of paper that gives the title to, or the interest in, a piece of real estate.

DEFAULT – This is what happens when someone does not repay their mortgage—they default on the loan.

DELINQUENT TAXES – This is what taxes are called when they are past due and not paid.

DEPRECIATION – This is the word that means that your property is losing its value.

DUAL AGENCY – This is what it is called when the same agent is the agent for both the buyer and the seller.

EARNEST MONEY DEPOSIT – This is the money given to the seller by the buyer to indicate their interest in buying the house.

EASEMENT – This is the legal right to use a piece of land that someone else owns for a set purpose. The little chunk of land that sits between the curb and the sidewalk is the city's easement; they own it but they allow you to use it.

EMINENT DOMAIN – This is the term heard when the government wants to build something and they want your property. The government has the right to eminent domain, which means that they can buy your property for the bare minimum price and make you move off of it if they want to use that land for something else.

ENCUMBRANCE – This is anything that will lower the value of the property such as an unpaid tax bill or an unpaid lien from a past owner.

EQUITY – This is the monetary difference between how much you owe and how much the house is worth. This is money that you can use to buy more properties.

ESCROW – This is an account set up at a bank that holds money that will be used to pay the mortgage payment and sometimes the insurance and the taxes.

EVIDENCE OF TITLE – This is the actual proof that you own the property. This would be a title abstract with the lawyer's opinion, a title insurance policy, or a certificate of title.

EXPENSES – These are the costs that are associated with keeping up the property such as maintenance fees and minor repairs.

FEATURES – These are like amenities for the house, things like garages, pools, hot tubs, and decks.

FHA LOAN – This is a loan that is guaranteed by the Federal Housing Administration. It will be made to the buyer by a lender that is approved by the FHA and in accordance with FHA guidelines.

FIRST MORTGAGE – The mortgage that makes a superior lien against the house and gets paid first before any other mortgage

FIXED RATE MORTGAGE – This is the type of mortgage that has one rate of interest for the entire life of the loan.

FIXTURE – This is a piece of personal property that was in some way attached to the house and is now a part of the house, like a lighting fixture or an appliance.

FORECLOSURE – This is a legal proceeding where the property that is being used as the security for a mortgage loan is sold in order to pay the mortgage loan when the buyer defaults or can't pay the mortgage.

FRAUD – This is when a material fact is not stated correctly so that it seems to mean something else or stand for something else.

GENERAL CONTRACTOR – This is the person who joins into a formal contract to do construction on the property of another person. The job of the general contractor will be to ensure that all of the work is completed and he will often hire other people to do certain jobs for him.

HOME WARRANTY – This is an insurance policy that will cover systems in the house and big-ticket items, like the HVAC, the roof, and the appliances. If one of them needs repair or replacing you will pay a small deductible and the insurance company will pay the remainder.

IMPROVEMENT – This is something that is done to the property that makes the property more valuable.

INDUSTRIAL PROPERTY – This is property that is suitable for and used for distribution, storage, and production of various goods.

INSPECTION – This is the survey that is taken of the home by a licensed home inspector. This report will tell you about any problems the inspector notices that may require a large outflow of cash to repair.

INSURANCE – This is what you pay for that will repay you if there is a loss on the property, like a fire or a tree falls into the house.

INTEREST – This is the money paid for the privilege of borrowing money.

LEASE – This is the contract that is written between the landlord (lessor) and the tenant (lessee) for the purpose of living in the house. The lease gives the tenant the legal right to use the house and the property for a pre-set amount of time in exchange for a certain amount of monthly payments that he will pay to the landlord.

LESSEE – This is the tenant who rents the house.

LESSOR – This is the landlord or owner who rents the house to the tenant.

LIABILITY – This is something that you owe to someone else, like a bill.

LIEN – This is the right that is given to creditors who have done work to a house and not been paid for their work.

LIQUIDITY – This is being able to sell an owned asset and turn it into ready cash money.

LISTING – This is the term that means a house for sale or the actual ad that tells about a house for sale.

LISTING AGENT – This is the seller's agent who will list the home for sale and do their best to find a buyer.

LISTING AGREEMENT – This is the agreement made between the seller and the real estate agent where the seller agrees that the real estate agent will be the one who sells their home and the real estate agent agrees to sell the house for the seller.

MARKET PRICE – This is the price that the property actually sells for.

MARKET VALUE – This is the price that the market sets which is the price that the seller would sell at and the buyer would buy at.

MORTGAGE – This is the money that is borrowed in order to be able to buy a property.

MORTGAGE BROKER – This is the person who will take care of all the detail between the lender and the borrower.

MUNICIPAL ORDINANCES – These are the codes, regulations, and laws that are made and enforced by the local or state government.

NOTARIZE – This is a process where a notary public certifies the signatures on a document and the validity of a document.

OFFER – This is the price the buyer says they will pay the seller in order to be able to buy the house.

PAYEE – This is the person who gets the payment.

PAYOR – This is the person who gives the payment.

PERSONAL PROPERTY – This is property that is not real estate; it is movable and can be taken from one place to another.

PRE-APPROVAL LETTER – This is a letter the buyer can get from the bank that will tell the seller how much they have been told they can get a loan for.

PREPAYMENT PENALTY – This is a clause that is written into a note that makes an extra charge on the customer when they pay the note off early. This clause is to make up for things like interest that the lender is losing.

PRINCIPAL – This is the amount of money that someone borrows in order to buy a house. When you pay off principal then you will build equity.

PRIVATE MORTGAGE INSURANCE – This is an insurance policy that some people will need to buy to pay to the lender so that the lender is protected in case the buyer can't pay the loan back.

PROPERTY MANAGER – This is a person who will manage your property for you so that you can spend your time growing your empire.

REAL ESTATE AGENT – This is a person who has a license that allows them to help people find houses to buy and to sell.

REFINANCING – This happens when you get a new loan to pay off your current mortgage loan. When you refinance, it is usually so that you can get a lower monthly payment or a lower rate of interest.

TITLE INSURANCE – This is insurance that will cover the title of the home in case something appears later to challenge whether or not you are holding a valid title.

These are certainly not all of the terms that you will come into contact with while you are building your real estate empire but they are some of the more common ones. Always ask a trusted person if there is something you do not understand. Your local library will probably have many books that will help you understand exactly what it is you are doing, and best of all they are free to borrow.

So learn your terms and create your business plan and start looking for that first wonderful property that will become the basis of the marvelous portfolio that you will grow. This is an exciting time in your life. You are beginning to make the plan that will carry you well into the future and give you the basis you need for a satisfying self-made career.

CONCLUSION

Thank you for making it through to the end of Rental Property Investing: Secrets of a Real Estate Building Empire: Principles to Make 7 Figures of a Passive Income Establishing a Real Estate Investment Empire. Let's hope it was informative and able to provide you with all of the tools you will need to achieve your goals whatever they may be.

The next step is to start. Grab a notebook and write down a plan for where you want to be in one year, five years, and ten years. Your first year will be the beginning of your empire and it may not go exactly as you plan but you will learn and you will grow. Take what you learn on the first few houses and build on that until you build the portfolio of your dreams. Try to stay well-grounded but don't be afraid to take a few risks. And do not ever stop trying. You will reach your goal.

Finally, if you found this book useful in any way, a review on Amazon is always appreciated!

JONATHAN FITZPATRICK

SIGN UP!

Visit our website:

WWW.JONATHANFITZPATRICKAUTHOR.COM

and enter you email address to receive exclusive bonus contents related to the updates of this book and find out everything about Jonathan Fitzpatrick's new publications, launch offers and other exclusive promotions!

PASSIVE INCOME

THE HOLY GRAIL OF FINANCIAL FREEDOM

The Side Hustle Blueprint to Learn How to Make
Money Without Being Actively Involved

JONATHAN FITZPATRICK

PASSIVE

INCOME

THE HOLY GRAIL OF FINANCIAL FREEDOM

THE SIDE HUSTLE BLUEPRINT TO LEARN HOW TO MAKE MONEY WITHOUT BEING ACTIVELY INVOLVED

JONATHAN FITZPATRICK

DISCLAIMER

The information contained in this book is for general information and educational purposes only. This book assumes no responsibility for errors or omissions in the contents on the Service.

This book have no liability for any damage or loss (including, without limitation, financial loss, loss of profits, loss of business or any indirect or consequential loss).

 JONATHAN FITZPATRICK

SIGN UP!

Visit our website:

WWW.JONATHANFITZPATRICKAUTHOR.COM

and enter you email address to receive exclusive bonus contents related to the updates of this book and find out everything about Jonathan Fitzpatrick's new publications, launch offers and other exclusive promotions!

INTRODUCTION

Hi, I am Jonathan Fitzpatrick, a young online entrepreneur. In my first three years of business, I was able to increase my passive income from zero to seven figures by applying different model business.

I started with Amazon FBA and went from zero to six figures annually in my first twelve months of activity. Once I had stabilized, I had integrated a second source of passive income through a business called affiliate marketing. Today I am also a real estate investor, and I earn seven figures a year through these different passive business models

WHAT IS PASSIVE INCOME OR AS IT IS SOMETIMES KNOWN – RESIDUAL INCOME?

Simply put, it is a receivable you get, even if you are not actively working. It is important to understand that income is different from salary - Income is all that someone receives, whereas, salary is what you get through work, i.e., sale of time.

Passive income means a way to raise resources without the need for the physical presence of the recipient of this income, i.e., money comes in regardless of what the recipient of this income is doing. It is tied to the idea of putting money to work for you, not the other way around.

Now, if you want to ensure a peaceful future, it is important to start generating passive income because that can bring you more security and stability. Understanding the definition of passive income as creating a system that will generate income without (or with little) work, will help you build a better future. The next step is to try and create a passive income, but what if you have no money? Do not worry, that can be taken care of too. It is not easy, but with determination and enough effort, it is possible (and relatively cheap). Let's take a look at the different (and economical) ways to generate passive income.

SECTION

ONE

LEARNING ONLINE METHODS TO EARN PASSIVE INCOME

CHAPTER 1
AFFILIATE MARKETING

Now that we have defined what passive / residual income is, let's define what an affiliate marketing / program is.

Affiliate Marketing is a type of marketing done by sites that register webmasters or people to advertise their banners or links on their websites or on the internet. The webmasters register for free in the affiliate programs offered by these sites and start to divulge a special link, banner, window or any type of advertisement, originated from its register (usually with a personal code embedded). It is a type of result marketing where the webmaster or affiliate of the site only receives money or premium for clicks, impressions or sales originating from your code.

There are several types of affiliate programs like CPC, CPA and CPM. Each of these types generates a certain type of feedback to the user. CPC, or Cost Per Click, generates a return whenever a person clicks on an affiliate program link. CPA, or Cost-per-Action, generates a return whenever a person buys a product or service within a program. CPM, or Cost Per Thousand, generates a profit for every thousand banners displayed on the affiliate's website.

1 - SITES WITH ADVERTISING BANNERS - GOOGLE ADSENSE

If you have a blog or website, which has Google advertising banners, you can win with every click. Some people create blogs or sites and position them well in the search engines, just to place these banners and make money with Google Adsense.

2- AFFILIATE MARKETING FOR COMPANIES

Another way is to advertise other companies/tools and make money as an affiliate. For example, you use a hosting service that you love, make a post or place a banner with your affiliate link and then, with every person that hires this hosting service, you get a percentage. This way, you can make money with every sale or subscription of the product that comes from your site.

3- AFFILIATE MARKETING WITH CONTENT MARKETING

This is one of my favorites. After all, this is what I do. To understand this, let's say that you make a video or blog post talking about a certain product and leave your affiliate link there. Every day, at least one new person gets to know about your work, and that content keeps being on air for years, generating passive income.

4- CREATING DIGITAL PRODUCTS

When we are talking about generating passive income through the internet, another viable option is to create a digital product that does not need support, such as an e-book where the person buys it to read it and by extension, any other digital product that does not need support to generate income. I gave the e-book example because it is simple to create – it's just like a book, only digital.

5 - MINI SITES

These are sites focused only on a specific subject and are very well-positioned in Google and other search engines. They have a great SEO. Within these sites, you can have e-books for sale, or any other digital product that you have created or own. It's like a direct page talking about just one product. For example, in the above option, we talk about if you create an e-book, then it is possible to create a mini-site and make it available for purchase. Every person who enters Google and search for that subject can find your page (mini site) and buy the product.

6- BUYING A SITE THAT IS ALREADY YIELDING

There are sites that have already been on air, for a certain time. They are already making money with Google Adsense. Now, it is possible to invest in such sites and continue to win. In other words, you pay for this site only once, and then generate passive income, if you want, you can work on this site to include new information, work further on SEO and earn even more.

7- CREATE TEMPLATES OR PHOTOS TO SELL

If you understand the subject, it is possible to assemble templates and make them available on several template-selling websites. And the same thing works with photos; if you like taking pictures, you can make money from that also, providing images of food, travel, among many other subjects.

CHAPTER 2
BLOGGING

W hen talking about passive income, we have to talk about one of the best and most popular ways of generating the same – Blogging. How to make money with a blog even without having a huge audience (avoid the biggest mistakes made by amateurs). The fact of having a blog without ads always instigated people's curiosity: how can it be possible to make money from a blog without depending on clicks?

Honestly speaking, if you go along with the strategy of making money from blogs through ads, you will come to know that the effectiveness of this type of strategy only decreases year after year. The problem with this monetization model is that you need an absurd amount of ongoing traffic to generate some income. This applies to your website or blog as well as to your YouTube channel.

In addition to losing the power to generate revenue, a blog full of ads hinders the navigation of its readers, resulting in a terrible experience. The obvious question which comes up next is – "Is there another way to make money through a blog?". I'll say – "Yes, of course!"

To let you know how to make money from blogging, we'll go point by point and learn about things which are extremely crucial for this strategy to succeed.

1. WHY INBOUND MARKETING IS BETTER, AND WHY DO WE NEED IT?

If you watch videos on YouTube, you must have been through this unpleasant situation where you're paying attention to the content of the video, and suddenly, without warning, an ad begins streaming in the middle of your video. Irritating, right? In addition to displaying ads at the beginning of the videos, stopping the user in between is, in my opinion, one of the worst ways to get attention.

These advertising pop-ups, so to say, play a disruptive role and may rightly be called as misplaced or overkill ads, among others. That interruption method, the basis of Outbound Marketing or Old Marketing still works, no doubt. However, this aggressive and intrusive strategy has been losing more and more relevance. We're basically so accustomed to seeing ads scattered everywhere that we do not pay attention to them anymore.

Inbound Marketing, on the other hand, does not allow you to buy or interrupt the attention of your audience. Your strategy is based on gaining interest. A clear example of this is when you decide to subscribe to a list of emails. Inbound Marketing presents results far superior to Outbound or Old Marketing, especially in Digital Marketing, being responsible for 90% of the clicks on the web and presenting a low cost in the acquisition of a new client.

2. HOW TO WIN THE TRUST OF YOUR AUDIENCE?

The main point of this is: if you just focus on selling and you do not like what you do, and you're not really worried about your audience, people will notice. And they will not trust you! However, if you can gradually win the trust of your readers through quality articles and tips that help them solve problems, they will put you on a higher level in your "trust meter", and the more opportunities to sell a product / service you will have because they know you are not pushing something., but offering a way to solve a problem, an affliction or lack of knowledge.

3. TRAFFIC – IS IT NECESSARY? IS IT ENOUGH?

I'll be honest: It is necessary. It is not enough. And even so, generating an avalanche of traffic is no easy task. Especially if you are creating your first blog, the beginning can be frustrating. Some take months and months to begin to reap the results of your efforts. Others end up giving up halfway, believing they will not succeed.

But you do not have to have a list of 150,000 registered or reach the threshold of 8 million visits to start understanding how to make money with a blog. Now, other than ads spread across the blog (we have already talked about this), there is one other way to make money through blogs: Ads and posts sponsored by major brands. This also depends on an absurd amount of traffic. They look for people who have significant numbers of followers on social networks and a number of at least 100,000 monthly hits on the blog, depending on the niche.

After all, the more people who access that content, the greater the reach of the brand in relation to the final audience. And the higher your audience, the higher the price you can charge for this type of post.

In addition to the high traffic requirement, by investing only in this monetization model, you will be dependent on the interest of other companies in you and your blog may still displease your audience, so it's not enough.

4. AFFILIATE MARKETING – THE NEXT STEP
As mentioned above, Affiliate Marketing works like this:

You join a product. You place your affiliate link on your website or any other media. A user clicks on your link and falls on the product page being promoted. He buys the product, and you earn a commission for the sale.

Now, this is a good way to make money from blogging that did not involve clicks on Adsense ads. Of course, by betting on Affiliate Marketing as a source of income, you cannot go out selling anything. The effect will be exactly the same as crowding your banner site: your audience will lose confidence in you.

So, follow some basic rules: Indicate only those products that you trust and use, maintain consistency with the niche of your blog, and please state that this is an affiliate link to keep it transparent.

5. SELL YOUR OWN PRODUCTS

In the above approach, there is a lot of work which includes: Market research, search for data sources, a mental map of ideas, content generation, hiring a designer, strategy of dissemination and creation of a sales page. In addition, search for partnerships, interviews, integration between sales page and distribution and marketing of info-product, support to new customers. The gain is much greater when you are the creator of the product. However, the work grows to the same extent.

In my opinion, it's a step that every digital entrepreneur who wants to make money with a blog needs to give in a moment. Not to mention that this is not an exclusive choice. You can merge the two strategies for even better results.

6. EXCLUSIVE CONTENT FOR MEMBERS

Many people like to have access to unique content to feel that they have something that most people do not have. And if you can get a loyal audience, who trusts your work, you would surely find people willing to pay a monthly fee to gain access to a little more of your content.

You can create a member-only content area on your blog by making a recurring monthly payment and offering both articles, videos, and PDF materials.

7. INVISIBLE SELLING THROUGH PERSUASIVE CONTENT

When you start selling over the internet, you will find one of the biggest barriers: resistance to sale. In today's world, people have grown accustomed to getting free content on the internet. And many feel truly offended if they need to pay to get something. So you already must assume that people are not ready to buy while consuming content over the internet.

To be characterized as an invisible sale, your recommendation regarding a particular product or service should sound exactly what it is: a recommendation. You already create a connection with the reader and deliver content of value throughout the article. Then, you make a single call to action at the end of the article.

8. ANTICIPATING YOUR AUDIENCE'S WANTS AND NEEDS

Are you a committed fan of any TV series? If so, I think you're pretty anxious when the next season's release date is coming up. This feeling of dreaming about what we cannot have now is fuelled by the trigger of anticipation. This is extremely powerful because it activates parts of the brain linked to happiness, in addition to leaving your reader eager for the upcoming sale. For this reason, it is so used for any type of release. You can make a series of articles, infographics or videos to generate curiosity in your audience. This is the first part of an internet launch.

9. THE TIME TO SHOW YOURSELF AND YOUR PRODUCT

You've done all the work in anticipation. Now is the time to present your product / service through a sales video. It is at this point that you need to reinforce why you are offering your knowledge to people. As well as the results they should expect with their product. Through a well-defined mission that motivates you to share your experience through a product / service and a strong background story, you will gain more public confidence.

CHAPTER 3
LEAD GENERATION WEBSITE

Generating leads from a blog or website is where the financial return of an advertising campaign occurs. Some of the readers click and buy what we are indicating, others click and register in the advertiser's site or simply by clicking. This reader action, if we have a good lead generation strategy in practice, can be encouraged without you having to ask your readers to do so. In the following paragraphs, we are going to discuss some strategies to increase these conversions and make your campaigns highly profitable.

HOW TO WORK WITH CAMPAIGNS FOCUSED ON LEAD GENERATION?

What perhaps many bloggers and webmasters have not yet realized is that they have unlimited spaces for advertising on their blogs and websites. Few realize that the best way of lead generation is to indicate commissioned products and services that are related to the content of their articles. If they use their articles as a weapon in lead generation, their advertising space is unlimited.

Of course, with this type of indication, one must always be very careful not to indicate products and services that are not of good quality for their readers, as they are using their image for this indication and, over time, they might lose credibility if they do not recommend relevant products and services. Therefore, indicating products and services that are related to the content of your articles, is one of the better ways to take as you will also be complementing the need of your readers.

CHAPTER 4
CONTENT CURATOR

It is risky to say that we are at the height of the information age; after all, technology is evolving so rapidly that the future becomes unpredictable. However, it is not difficult to see that we are increasingly surrounded by information and content, especially with the advent of social media, and it is common to find people with difficulties to manage them.

When an entrepreneur decides to bet on content marketing, basically he will have two options: The creation or replication of information present on the web, a process normally done through social media or email marketing. However, when you choose to perform only the second option, you will soon encounter some difficulties. After all, what content really can be relevant to my audience and to my business? It is precisely to solve this type of question that a content curation becomes necessary.

The process involves segmenting and filtering content for later delivery to the target audience, through sharing on accessible channels. To get an idea, every 60 seconds, 168 million emails are sent worldwide, 600 videos are posted on Youtube, and 1500 texts are posted on blogs. Another point that makes curation even more relevant is the fact that content cannot simply be "thrown" into networks without contextualization. Now, this brings us to the next question -

How to curate content? There is a model for conducting a curation, which is divided into three stages:

1. The research, which consists of monitoring news and articles and identifying the best sources. There are several online tools that help the curator's work - we'll talk about them next! The use of Google alerts and RSS feeds from relevant blogs can also be extremely useful to keep yourself constantly updated.

2. Contextualization: As already mentioned, it is important to give meaning to what is published, according to the interests of the company and the profile of the target audience. Through social media feedback, it is possible to evaluate what is working.

3. Last, but not least, we go to the sharing phase, and here we must define through which channels it will be realized.

Searching for links, blog articles, and web-based information that seems relevant and useful to your audience seems like a time-consuming process. However, there are several ways to optimize this work, making this task much more automated and with more accurate results for your marketing.

Firstly, use social networks. Yes, your company's social networks can be a way to filter good content and know which topics are relevant to your marketing. The two most relevant platforms for good curation are Facebook and Twitter - and even if your company does not use Twitter, it can benefit from the site's filtering and search tools. The social network is increasingly investing in relevant and current content filtering in their research.

Secondly, use Social Media Marketing Kits and Tools to filter content by relevance. Example, BuzzSumo is a site that helps you analyze and filter relevant content through topic search. It selects the results of each keyword searched through the number of shares and backlinks of each article and news - exactly the factors that will help you decide the social impact on the Web. This is the favorite tool for several major brands and content producers.

Thirdly, calibrate your searches by content through tools like Social Mention, which focus on blogging and microblogging publications - especially Twitter. This tool helps you better calibrate your search by content, offering the best keyword suggestions related to your search, and finding users who may have shared articles and news relevant to your content marketing.

Other useful tools include Pocket, to store discovered content, and Feedly, to find and organize RSS, etc. Now you already know what content curation is, how it can be beneficial to your marketing and the main tools for the curator. But, to be a successful curator, I am mentioning some of the tips which have been found useful by a lot of people.

1. DO NOT TALK TOO MUCH, BUT RATHER TOO LITTLE

One of the most common mistakes when making a Curatorship is to look for topics and topics in excess. This makes your curation very broad, and the information found will never be treated with continuity and depth.

2. KEEP FREQUENCY WITH YOUR CURATORS

There is no point in starting a curation of content if there is no way to keep this curatorial active over time, right? Check out an interesting frequency - daily, weekly, bi-weekly - for content search and always have new and relevant information for your marketing and business at hand.

3. USE ONLY THE TOOLS AND HABITS THAT HELP YOU.

Another quite common misconception - and little pointed - in companies that begin to perform curatorship is an insistence on what does not work for the team. Often, the professional in charge of the marketing industry requires the use of tools or habits that simply are not productive for the team. Therefore, seek together with your co-workers the forms and tools most adaptable to the reality of your work.

The next question which will be popping up in your mind right now would be – "How to Choose the Right Content for My Content Marketing Strategy?"

Start with the sales funnel. What kind of material will help with conversions at each step of the funnel? You can find a lot of good content that will support your sales funnel and for the buying journey. Then, look at the top questions the sales team faces when finalizing a sale. It is common to have doubts throughout the process, and evergreen content is the perfect solution to answer the questions of your business opportunities. Think about the information you need for your strategy and go after them! Keywords are great for these searches since it is through them that visitors will get to your blog.

Now, onto the final step, how to take good advantage of the content (after you've done the curation). It's no use finding quality material if you're going to leave it in some lost folder of your favorites. Good content needs to be shared with the world!

As we have already said, social media is the first option - and one of the most important - but the buck does not stop there. Email marketing campaigns and newsletters are also excellent vectors for this content, especially if your list is stuffed with quality contacts. And, do not forget LinkedIn. Even though it is a social network, it has a slightly different approach to others. You can create posts in there, and share in groups related to your area of expertise.

Lastly, remember the credit! In content marketing, if you have one thing that is very important is credit! A large part of replicating relevant content is giving credit to the original author by linking to the article and showing to the reader where it was originally posted.

CHAPTER 5
PRICE COMPARISON WEBSITE

This is one of the ways which became popular along with the advent of various e-commerce portals online. Now, the question which stands tall here is - How to enter your virtual store on this channel? Let's say that you already have a good store, offer good products and can reach a good customer base. Your profit comes in every month, but you're still not happy. On the contrary, you want to show everyone that you have a good, efficient, low-priced store and that within your niche, it can present itself as the best option in the market. Well, a good way for you to make it happen is to be able to enter your e-commerce within the price comparison site.

There's more than one way to get your merchandise to come to appear on the internet. One of the most desired by those who bet on the cost-benefit of the products they sell is the insertion of their website into price comparators.

WHAT MAKES THE PRICES COMPARATOR SITES?

If you buy from the internet with some frequency, I'm sure you would've already learned how to search on price comparators. That is, you get the product you want to score, with all your main technical specifications and you play on the internet.

Price comparison sites will assign within a series of websites which offer the lowest prices found. This is an efficient way to carry out screening. With this tool, the user quickly identifies which are the best buying options for that product. Examples include sites such as Shopbot, Buscapé, Shopping Uol , Bondfaro or Google Shopping.

These systems work as a kind of product disclosures and compare the prices among several different electronic trades. The main advantage of them is obvious: they aggregate countless visitors who wish to buy a particular commodity. That way, you buy a package on a price comparator website already knowing with complete certainty the qualification it will give the visitor.

PAGES FOR COMPARED PRICE SITES ARE A GOOD MARKETING OPTION

These pages that compare product prices are nothing more than a marketing option, which, although practical, play a very important role so that you do not give up on a strategy and make sure you constantly monitor your products to make sure your proposal has worked. To do this, you must always analyze the number of clicks and also, always, calculate the rate of return on investment (ROI).

Only then will the shopkeeper be able to know exactly what is the next decision that will need to be made to establish themselves in the market. Another important point to note is the need for price comparison, websites will not be held responsible, in any kind of hypothesis, for the content of the advertisement in question. Thus, it is essential that you convey, through the description of the products and the photos as the product really is, giving the buyer a sense of security and credibility.

YOUR SITE NEEDS TO HAVE A WELL RESOLVED LAYOUT

If you want to reach a wider range of customers, then keeping in mind the fact that the vast majority of price comparators only work effectively with those tenants who own a website, you need to have a beautiful, practical and functional page. If your site is confusing, slow and poorly structured, it is almost certain that the customer will give up the purchase or not feel safe enough to make the purchase through this channel. As has been emphasized before, one of the essential points for your business to progress is that you can convey a credibility of security and trust to the customer.

INVEST IN SECURITY

To emphasize the above topic, you need to obtain security certificates, such as SSL for HTTPs or certifications such as e-Bit. You need to keep in mind that no shopper will think of buying at a store if it goes through your mind that he may have problems putting his personal information in that store to buy a product.

KNOW THE RULES AND PROHIBITIONS OF THE PLATFORMS

In order for your site to work in price comparators, you need to know all the prohibitions and rules of the platforms. For example, you cannot put photos that do not fit reality, and you cannot redirect the client to a site that was not previously informed. These platforms understand this type of situation as characteristics of those who seek to cause fraud and harm customers. So if you do this, you may end up being barred from putting your goods on that kind of platform that compares prices.

CHAPTER 6
DIGITAL BUSINESS INVESTOR
(INVESTING IN ESTABLISHMENT ONLINE BUSINESS)

The internet is very democratic, and for this reason, it is possible to create online businesses of the most varied types, of the most varied purposes and aimed at the most varied public. There is room for all kinds of ideas, with a good deal of willpower and preparation, a person will be able to set up their business online without having to spend a lot of money. Little Investment and Absurd Results! But what do you need to succeed?

Simply put, Strategy Is Everything You Need!

The great secret of those who already know how to make money online is simply to bet all their main chips in a good strategy since the strategy is everything within the digital entrepreneurship. Knowing the best strategies of digital marketing and knowing exactly the right time to apply each one of them can be the most determining factor for your digital business to grow.

With much will and study, you can learn how to make money online in a short time, and you can create a digital business that is profitable and able to bring you all the return you want. So believe me when I say that anyone can become a digital entrepreneur. Anyone can get this done and make lots of money on the internet without leaving home.

To start with, let me tell you about some tips and ways in which you can make money by investing in digital businesses. (Of course, you'll need to invest in knowledge and follow the best strategy pertaining to particular channels). Some of these have already been mentioned and discussed in detail in the earlier chapters of this book.

1. MAKE MONEY WITH BLOGS

The recipe for making money from blogs is simple: Create quality content related to the products or services you want to promote and place sales on "autopilot" using the affiliate programs. As emphasized earlier, there are some cautions when setting up a professional blog:

First, define the niche market that will work, preferably some subject that understands and dominates. It's not a rule, but it helps a lot. Then you can create the blog, write articles related to the subject that will be addressed and finally monetize your project by indicating and recommending the products through affiliate links. Lastly, you need to create your audience, generate massive traffic on your blog, or you risk writing and no one reading, which in addition to being frustrating, will not bring profits.

2. EARN MONEY WITH GOOGLE ADSENSE

Here is already another strand of digital marketing using blogs to monetize your projects. The creation of the blog is very similar to the one mentioned in our first tip, but in this case, you will not indicate any product. Briefly, blogging about making money using Google Adsense, needs many articles and strategic spaces on the site so that the ads appear on the screen of your readers, and they click easily. You will win per click. However, you need to be cautious that you don't overkill it, as has been warned before. If you ask me personally, I would say I prefer the first option over this one.

Some other things which you can keep in mind while investing in this:

a. Articles have to be well written using on-page SEO techniques and need to be large, at least 500 words.

b. Not all niches work with Google Adsense, choose niches that have many visits.

c. Create lots of articles and do heavy SEO work because this type of monetized site only yields profits if you have a lot of organic traffic.

d. Always optimize your projects by choosing the correct places to place the ads and tracking the click metrics.

3. HOW TO MAKE MONEY ON FACEBOOK

Here we already enter a world half parallel to blogs. Social Networks, especially Facebook, can be a good place to look at how to make money on the Internet. The fastest way to make money on Facebook is by advertising on Facebook

Ads, in which case you will need to invest in generating traffic on your affiliate links.

Briefly create publications on your timeline or on fan pages indicating a product or service for people to buy and all distribution of this content is made through Facebook through sponsored ads.

4. GENERATE INCOME WITH SEO

In a nutshell SEO is the set of techniques that aim to position a website in the first places in search engine results, especially Google. You can do this work on your own projects, ranking your sites, generating organic traffic and free. You can also do SEO work professionally by offering this type of service to other people or companies that have an interest in positioning your websites well in the search engines. These SEO techniques go far beyond writing optimized content, in fact the biggest job is the SEO Offpage (Creating External Links).

5. MAKE MONEY ON YOUTUBE

This tip could not be left out, YouTube is now the second largest source of organic traffic on websites and blogs, it has great visibility, and many people prefer watching videos than reading articles. The 3 popular ways (not exhaustive) to make money with Youtube videos:

a. Create videos on miscellaneous topics and monetize on Youtube Adsense.

b. Create daily videos and become a Youtuber, achieving marketing contracts with large companies.

c. Create short videos explaining the characteristics of some product and indicating your affiliate links.

I suggest you choose only one of these ways to make money online and focus on it because at the beginning, too much information can cause confusion and if you do not have focus, you will have problems. Once you get your first profits on the internet, you can expand your digital business and multiply your results. But, do remember – invest in knowledge and follow a tried and tested strategy – only then will you be able to excel in this area.

CHAPTER 7
LOCAL BUSINESS MARKETER
(SOCIAL MEDIA MARKETING)

Many local businesses are unable to visualize themselves in the midst of Inbound Marketing and Content Marketing. The reason? To think that they are methodology incompatible with their realities and that the benefits are clearer for businesses of national scope. However, several local enterprises that started investing in this mindset have had concrete results, proving that the model works. One can use the strategies wisely to deliver results for diverse local businesses.

We have some cases of local companies that used, among the various strategies of Inbound Marketing, the content marketing to aid in this gain of scale – Douglas Lima, Koetz Advocacy Office and many more. The interesting thing, and what you may realize, is that such strategies work for companies from different niches. Photography, advocacy, dentistry and wine trade have already confirmed that it is possible to generate great results with practice. Other segments are possible as well. One just needs to invest money and time wisely.

So, even if the company is a local business that depends on people's on-site visit, making use of content marketing can generate quite impressive results. In addition to being a viable strategy for local SEO, it also serves to nourish an audience by creating a community of loyal customers.

You can use Inbound marketing (specifically in cases of local businesses) to educate the audience and potential customers; be a reference in a certain subject related to your market; and influence the purchase decision.

Check out a few steps you need to take into consideration to start thinking about your content marketing strategy:

1. POSITION YOURSELF!

First of all, you must think about the persona that your company wants to reach, the desired positioning and the type of content that makes the most sense to be published.

Does your client need to learn about the topic? This is often the case in health, wine, law, fashion, among other areas. People have curiosities and doubts about subjects they are interested in, and they like to receive tips on these topics.

Is your work interesting in itself? Often, photos of how the weekend was at a ballad or bar already help generate interest and comments. If it is still none of the above, what is interesting and is around your market? The calendar of events of the city in the week for a taxi co-op? The latest football news for a sports bar? The latest releases of music videos and songs for an alternative ballad?

2. TRY TO CAPTURE THE CONTACT OF THE VISITORS

Create ways to collect the emails of your users. Whether through blogging, landing pages, or contact forms, keep in mind that those users who are entering their email somewhere on your site are potential buyers of your product or service. There are endless ways to convert your visitors into leads. In blog posts you can have a field to subscribe to a newsletter. This can be at the end of the posts or even in the blog sidebar, in a popup or in the page footer.

Another way to capture these contacts is by creating rich materials and making them available for free download on a Landing Page. If you own a mechanic shop, you can create a checklist for the driver to do in the car before a trip. If you are a nutritionist, you can create a healthy eating guide for the summer. If it's a language school, you can create a quiz to test the knowledge of your visitors.

3. INVEST IN ADS TO TARGET THE EXACT AUDIENCE LOCALLY AND HAVE INITIAL TRACTION

It does not mean forgetting to work other techniques like SEO of your blog, for example. But investing in ads will give a traction, at least initially, to your business. Campaigns in Google Adwords or Facebook Ads have an incredible targeting factor, which is crucial for your local business or for your client's business.

4. KEEP ACCOUNTS ACTIVE IN SOCIAL NETWORKS AND PROMOTE YOUR CONTENT

People often look for stores on social media. This usually happens after they already know your business. So create the accounts using the name of your company, or if it is not possible, as close as possible. Social networking for local businesses can be important to do various actions like sweepstakes, contests, put information (menu, courses available, etc.), address and other things. In addition, of course, to be used for you to share the content produced.

Stats of 2019 show that over 40 million small businesses have pages on Facebook. Therefore, being on the largest social network on the planet is no longer a differential, but a basic aspect within Digital Marketing.

5. RELATIONSHIP

With a consolidated audience and leads generated, you need to think about how that relationship will be between your company and your customers. One advantage of using marketing automation is being able to create different streams for different audiences. That is, you can have a flow for sending newsletters and another for sending offers, coupons and promotions.

The important thing at this stage is to follow good email marketing practices to get the most out of it.

6. PLAN THE MEASUREMENT

Measure your actions online with efficiency is one of the biggest advantages of Digital Marketing. But how to measure when sales are offline? This is a fairly frequent question in face-to-face sales ventures, but there are a few existing solutions to clear up this nebulous issue.

As I said earlier too, the possibilities in the field of being a social media marketer (esp. for local businesses) are countless. With patience and good work done, the results should appear organically for your client's company in a few months.

CHAPTER 8
OUTSOURCED ONLINE SERVICE

What do people mean by this? Outsourcing services or Outsourced Online Services is a resource in which a company transfers to a third party, the responsibility in contracting and maintaining the legal relationship maintained with the employees. That is, it is the delegation of certain activities to another legal entity so that it fulfills with the execution of the labor tasks within its business.

Some business owners believe that outsourcing is a complex process and can create serious problems in the execution of internal activities. However, this thinking has changed, and outsourcing is becoming more and more accepted, even at the moment in which the legislation has expanded possibilities in the scope of services that can be contracted in this modality. Why will this attract a number of diverse clients?

COST REDUCTION
The first advantage is the one that attracts the most interest of the entrepreneurs: the reduction of costs. It is known that the labor charges, resulting from the correct application of the country's legislation, significantly affect companies, often causing a negative impact on the very development of activities.

By outsourcing, the relationship between cost and benefit is positive for the company's financial balance. This is because it involves costs lower than those required for the formation of a team and for the execution of activities within the business organization.

In addition to these issues, it is also worth mentioning that you can become specialized and offer professionals who have the greater technical knowledge, allowing productivity gain and, consequently, financial gain for the company. This is specifically important for those of you who are pretty experienced in one or two fields.

Finally, another indirect reduction of costs concerns the reduction of the structure of the Human Resources Department. This is because outsourcing causes a reduction in the demand for hiring, layoffs and the management of payroll and benefits paid to professionals.

TIME OPTIMIZATION

This is an interesting advantage related to the outsourcing process. This is because outsourcing allows the optimization of the time of managers and the professionals themselves since several operational activities are carried out by the companies that provide the services.

For example, the manager does not need to dedicate part of his time to preliminary interviews with candidates for a particular position, since the outsourced company will carry out the entire hiring process. In this sense, these professionals, as managers and directors, can focus the exercise of their functions in more strategic areas for the business. This allows for better decision making and, consequently, results.

PRIORITIZATION OF INVESTMENTS

The fact that a company elects to contract outsourced activities allows greater prioritization of investments for the organization. This is because outsourcing reduces the need for expenses with training and qualification of professionals since this task becomes a responsibility of the outsourcer.

This gives the company the possibility to prioritize its investments. Thus, you can privilege the use of your resources for strategies that are focused on the growth and development of the business.

SIMPLIFYING THE ADMINISTRATIVE STRUCTURE

This is a fairly obvious advantage when it comes to the benefits of outsourcing. It is natural for the company, when contracting outsourced employees, to guarantee the easy organization and management of cost control, optimizing investments, and avoiding problems related to administrative practices, impasses and even legal issues.

FOCUS ON HIRING EXPERTS

Another interesting benefit that is the Achilles heel of many organizations is the hiring of professional experts, and this is the major part where you as an outsourcer come in.

Outsourcing allows the hiring of more skilled and experienced employees. This circumstance guarantees the improvement in the quality of services and lower risks of hiring professionals who will not work efficiently and productively. This is because outsourcing companies usually invest in training and supplying professionals who stand out in their markets with specific skills and technical know-how.

All these reasons point to the obvious, the much widening gap and ever-increasing demand for outsourcers. One major thing which you need to keep in mind while monetizing this is not to diversify too much too early while entering the space. Quality work done with limited clients will go a long way in establishing your credibility and building a base for exponential growth in the future.

CHAPTER 9
JOB BOARD WITH A TWIST

The job board is the largest career website and gathers open opportunities in more than 3 thousand companies of the most varied segments. The service can bring many benefits to you who are looking for your first stage, or already have experience and need to relocate. If I were asked to list the main benefits of the job board, they would be the ones mentioned below:

1. YOU DO NOT NEED TO PAY ANYTHING

To use the services of you do not need to pay any fee. The registration is and always will be free for the candidates. Therefore, the site will never request your bank or credit card details.

2. YOU DO NOT FIND FALSE VACANCIES

The work is paid by the contracting companies - and never by the candidates. That's why all posts posted on the site are not real. After all, companies pay to make this publication, and it would not make sense for them to pay to advertise a vacant ghost, right?

3. YOU CAN USE THE SERVICE VIA THE APP

You can use the service for free also through the VAGAS app, available for Android and iOS systems. To download, go to the app store on your device and search for the term "VAGAS.com" or "Jobs."

4. YOU CAN SEARCH FOR VACANCIES IN ALL TYPES OF COMPANY

5. YOU CAN REFINE YOUR SEARCH

The search cannot be made from a job title or keyword, for example, "marketing analyst." The first results are presented in order of decreasing date, that is, from the most recent to the oldest. From there you can refine the search by city, country, areas of activity (Marketing, Administration, Communication, Engineering, for example), hierarchical level (junior / trainee, full, senior) and PCD.

6. YOU RECEIVE ALERTS OF VACANCIES IN YOUR E-MAIL

When a vacancy with your profile is published, you receive an alert directly in your e-mail, to register as soon as you can.

7. YOU CAN ACCESS YOUR APPLICATION HISTORY

In your registration, you have access to all your application history made by the site or the app.

8. YOU KNOW WHEN THE COMPANY HAS READ YOUR RESUME

To find out if your resume has been read on some application on the job board, you can check the viewing status in your history. Resumes read are flagged with the green icon "curriculum viewed."

9. YOU DO NOT NEED "IQ" (WHO INDICATES)

To compete for a place published in, you do not need the nomination of anyone. Just meet the ad's prerequisites and apply.

10. <u>YOU CAN FIND DETAILS ABOUT YOUR AREA OF WORK.</u>

It gives you important details about the positions, what you do, how much you earn and even the most frequent training of the people who work in these positions.

CHAPTER 10
CRYPTOCURRENCIES

C ryptocurrencies have come to revolutionize the way of doing business. We live in one of the best times to make money almost anywhere. The cryptocurrencies are one such example and they have come to transform the way of doing business and obviously making money.

On May 5, 2018, a tenth of a thousandth - four decimal places or 0.0001 - of a Bitcoin was worth about US $ 0.97, according to the CoinMarketCap, making now the best time to invest in Bitcoin and the crypto-coins. Learn more about this below.

1. <u>MICROTASKS TO WIN CRYPTOCURRENCIES</u>

This is an option that only requires you to have a computer and some free time. You can do some micro-tasking for someone or some service and win crypto coins in return. These microtasks can be something like downloading new applications for testing, watching videos, doing online surveys, etc. Some services that provide these are: microtasksBituro, Coin Bucks and Bitcoin Rewards

2. <u>BUY & HODL</u>

A safe way to make money online is to buy good crypto coins that have a fundamental use, case and keep them until you get fair market share. For example, crypto-coins like: Bitcoin, Ethereum, Litecoin, Monero and several others.

All of these are safe purchases most of the time. You can buy and hold them for a long term because they are

required to appreciate against the fiduciary pairs of USD, EUR, etc.

3. BUY AND HOLD CRYPTO COINS TO GET DIVIDENDS

Another smart way to win through Crypto Coins is to buy and keep Crypto Coins that pay dividends. There are many that give you a fair share just by guarding them and you are not even required to wager on them, especially in a wallet. Some of these crypto-coins are: NEO, COSS, KuCoin and CEFS

4. STAKING CRYPTOCURRENCIES

This is a great way to win, because you get the double benefit of price appreciation by owning good crypto coins, plus the additional reward of dividends for staking the coins. Staking is basically holding 24 × 7 crypto coins in a live wallet, thus gaining additional new coins as reward for staking and protecting the blockchain network.

5. MASTERNODES

The execution of masternodes of cryptocurrencies to obtain an intelligent passive income is also a way to win in the world of the cryptocurrencies. A masternode is simply a complete node of cryptocurrency or computer wallet that keeps the complete copy of the blockchain in real time, just as you have full Bitcoin nodes, and are always active to perform certain tasks. To perform such tasks, different networks of cryptomers pay the owners of the masternode.

6. DAY TRADING WITH CRYPTO-COINS

If you understand and are good at technical charts at various intervals of the day, this method of gain is for you. You can exchange different days of crypto coins in various trades. The idea is simple - buy low and sell high when you hit the target. This method works very well for a technical chart person because crypto coins, being a volatile market, can range from 20 to 50% in a day, depending on the choices you make.

7. WORKING FOR CRYPTO COINS

If you are a developer or a tester, a writer or a designer, you can start earning encrypted coins immediately by swapping your services for it. There are numerous platforms and sites that offer Bitcoins in exchange for their service.

8. ACCEPTING CRYPTO COINS IF YOU ARE A TRADER

Another way to make money online with crypto coins is to accept them in exchange for your products or services if you are a merchant. As a merchant, you have access to many Bitcoin crypto-coins and payment processors that can help you to accept them.

Even online business owners and e-commerce sites can adopt this form, thereby obtaining the double benefit of price enhancement of crypto-coins and earning crypto-coins directly.

In addition, in order to be able to mine and earn with crypto-coins, you must have access to cheap electricity to operate the mining equipment along with the technical know-how of how to take care of the software and hardware of the mining material.

CHAPTER 11
APP DEVELOPMENT

There is a lot of money involved in the application trade, billions of dollars. Certain types of applications are responsible for earning much of this money, while others are not able to generate much profit. The list of most profitable apps may be slightly different than you think. This chapter will explain all about how an application makes money and give you some ideas on how your application can become highly profitable.

The mobile market has grown considerably in recent years, and experts in this area expect continued growth. The use of the internet by mobile devices has surpassed the use by desktop in 2019, and more than 80% of Internet users have smartphones. With such impressive numbers, it is no surprise that large companies and investors want to join this world market.

If you are new to this market, you want to get into it or you just have an interesting idea for developing an application, one of the first things you should ask yourself is about the profitability of this investment. Developing an application is a difficult job, and you should want to be rewarded for all your work.

WHICH PLATFORM MAKES MORE MONEY FOR DEVELOPERS?

First and foremost, you need to choose which platform (or platforms) you want to use for the development of your application. This can significantly affect the potential for profit, as there is a difference in market presence and popularity. For this metric, let's evaluate the platforms based on the percentage of application developers earning at least $ 5,000 dollars per month for their applications.

The first place in this category is iOS, Apple's platform, with just over 25% of its developers making more than $ 5,000 a month. Android continues to be a great platform option because of its market presence index. 18% of Android developers earn more than $ 5,000 for their apps monthly. Despite this, it is worth noting that Android has a different form of profitability, since much of the total revenue coming from applications is the responsibility of the platform's top developers. The iOS platform, however, has a slightly more balanced division, increasing the chances of making money on this platform, even being a beginner.

Platforms that are not so favorable to people who want to make a profit from applications include the Blackberry operating system and the Windows mobile platform. The Blackberry does not have a market presence anywhere near iOS or Android, and its owner, RIM, sees its market share and financial gains declining annually. Windows has

Microsoft in its favor, but in the end, it's not as popular with smartphone users.

While niche platforms can generate a certain profit, they should only be considered after your application already generates income on more popular platforms. From the moment your application succeeds, it is more feasible to expand its performance to other platforms.

WHAT KIND OF INCOME DOES AN APP GENERATE?

Apps are great investments, and we cannot deny it. By 2018, global application market revenue reached $ 52 billion. That's around $ 10 billion more than 2017. Many experts predict growth of around 18% by 2020. Gaming applications dominate the list of most profitable applications. Bandai Namco Entertainment's Dragon Ball Z Dokkan Battle game has an estimated $ 2 million daily gain, while King Digital Entertainment's popular Candy Crush earns $ 1.6 million per day through in-app purchases. Supercell, the company behind the Clash of Clans and Clash Royale games, earns more than $ 2.3 billion annually.

HOW MUCH MONEY DO SUBSCRIPTION APPS EARN MONTHLY?

With more than 1 million subscribing users, Match Group's Tinder is a great example of an app that manages to make lots of money through in-house purchases. Tinder's relationship application has a free download but earns money by charging for bonus tools like Unlimited Likes, which gives users unlimited opportunities to get new combinations. The "plans" added to Tinder allow users to get new combinations from other locations, while boosts allow users to be able to make their profiles appear first to users in a certain area. In 2018, Match Group generated an estimated revenue of $ 285.3 million dollars. This new revenue model from Tinder has made it one of the most profitable applications worldwide.

On a smaller scale, individual applications are also capable of generating significant revenue. The Hooked application from The Telepathic earns around $ 2 million annually and is a relatively simple idea. Users can access suspense stories in the form of messages, through weekly, monthly, and yearly subscriptions. The app creates interest in users through interesting stories but requires a signature so they can figure out the ending.

The Kayla Itsines Swet with Kayla application serves as an example for novice application developers. The app offers 28-minute workouts and a diet. This app quickly gained users, generating something close to $ 45,100 dollars and approximately 9,000 users daily.

WHAT ARE THE NEXT TRENDS FOR APPLICATION DEVELOPMENT?

As you might note, there are several opportunities to get money in the application market. This market has managed to grow significantly since its inception and has no signs of slowing growth. Console applications can be able to generate a considerable income, but there is still plenty of room to grow within less complex and more popular platforms. And, finally, Smart TVs and Smart Watches still need to grow next to the consoles and will probably become part of the final expansion of this market until new devices come out in a concrete way.

CHAPTER 12
KDP

When it comes to publishing your first book on Amazon, it is normal to have butterflies in your stomach. To begin, let's talk about getting started on the book, and we'll take it from there. If you choose to write your own book, make sure you gather as much information about the subject in hand before you get started. It is important for you to gather all relevant information so that you are able to elaborate on every topic in detail and not miss out on anything.

Alternatively, you can choose to hire a writing agency to write a book for you. If you choose a writing agency, always give them all the information that you gathered so that you are both on the same page. This saves you a lot of time by avoiding going back and forth with editing, and it helps you to publish your book a lot faster. Once you have the content of your book covered, you need to decide on the cover for the book. You can get help from designers and freelancers that you can easily find on the Internet. If you prefer not to hand over the responsibility for the cover to someone else, you can always select a cover on the KDP website. Once you have uploaded the manuscript, you will get different options and be given a brief description of the eBook.

If you are looking for affordable services, Fiverr is a good choice. It has awesome covers starting at just $5, and you can get somebody to design a paperback and kindle cover for you at an affordable price. Once you get the cover sorted, tell them to give it to you in a PDF format, as this will help for when you are uploading the book on the Kindle publishing website. Once you have the content of your book sorted out and have a cover, it's time for you to publish your first ever book on Kindle Direct Publishing (KDP).

First, you need to sign up on KDP. Then, you need to select the title and sub-title of your eBook. Once that is done, you need to upload your eBook and the manuscript for the paperback design. The website is self-explanatory, so it's very easy for you just to follow the steps, get to the end, and finally publish your book on Amazon Kindle. It doesn't take a lot of time; in fact, your book could be live in just a few days!

We have spoken about people's preference for eBooks or paperbacks. However, there is a third type of people, the audiobook lovers. Some people prefer listening than reading because it's more convenient. Instead of missing out on this audience, get the help of ack.com, a sister company of Amazon. You don't even have to sign up on this website as you can use the same login details that you use on Amazon. Here, you can add a title for your book, look for it on Amazon and either upload the audio files already narrated by you, or ask them to do it for you. Audiobooks take a while to be produced, but they shouldn't be neglected as you manage to cover a section of people who prefer to listen to books and you leave yourself no room for error.

CHAPTER 13
FULFILLMENT BY AMAZON (FBA)

A nother popular method of earning money online is through FBA, which stands for Fulfillment by Amazon. It is an interesting platform that allows business owners to sell products on Amazon using the FBA platform. This platform basically enables buyers to choose products that can be delivered by Amazon. It is a popular method of online marketing because Amazon takes care of the shipping and delivery of a product thereby making it safer to trust. While this may seem extremely convenient for many people, it is one of the most complicated ways to earn money due to the amount of responsibility on your shoulders. Not only do you need to ensure that deliveries go out on time, but you also need to ensure that they are done in a precise manner and that there is no damage to any of the products. You get paid by Amazon depending on the delivery of a product. Also, you need to have your own space to store the product even if it is for a short time, and you are responsible for the packing of the product as well as returns. The pay-out for FBA is not that high, and there are more chances of making money with affiliate marketing.

When it comes to business owners, affiliate marketing is still the number one choice to promote products, for a number of reasons. One of the best things about affiliate marketing is that it is cost effective and as a business owner, you only need to pay for the number of products sold. It also helps create brand awareness in a more effective way.

Although some business owners still believe in advertisements on social media websites and search engines, none of these prove to be as effective as affiliate marketing because of the kind of exposure that the product gets with the publishers. This means that compared to other passive sources of income, affiliate marketing offers higher returns. This is because of the number of opportunities all around you. Affiliate marketing is not a complicated process as compared to the other ways to earn money online, and it happens to be the most convenient way as you do not have to worry about enhancing your skills or figuring out complicated programming or coding.

I started my entrepreneurial career online with Amazon FBA and my life has completely changed in just twelve short months.

More so, you would be envious of the amount of freedom I have to juggle and balance my personal and professional life. When was the last time I did something I love and enjoy? Well, I currently am. I love writing and disseminating knowledge. But if you are speaking in the realms of hobbies, then you should know that I do not miss any of my evening book club sessions. In fact, just yesterday afternoon I managed to attend a painting class, grab a drink with a friend and still managed to be home on time to read my niece a bedtime story. I believe that now I have your undivided attention.

These are the perks that have come with FBA. Fulfillment By Amazon. This is the gold mine that is little understood by those who know about it, let alone less publicized to the general public. For those who are quite familiar with the service, they understand that it is as simple as Buy; Ship; Receive Payment. Then why is it so complicated if it seems as natural.

Well, truth be told, FBA is rather intensive. Regardless of Amazon handling a huge chunk of the program, the bit left to the sellers is not a walk in the park. But I suppose that you already know this, and that is precisely why you are here. You understand what it takes to achieve your financial goals. With your primary goals set out, it will be a far easier job wading through these waters. Add that to an active and fueled mindset and a prosperous story is already being penned.

Fulfillment by Amazon (FBA) is often considered a subset of the dropshipping industry with a few major differences. Whereas with traditional dropshipping a third party is responsible for the sourcing and fulfilment of the orders, merchants in a Fulfilment by Amazon relationship send their items to Amazon who is then responsible for storing and shipping the items in question in return for a portion of the profits from the sale of the item. If you have an item that you are interested in creating a private label for but you weren't sure where the items were going to be stored or how you were going to find time to fill all of your future orders, then FBA is the answer.

In addition to making the physical transaction part of an online sale much less of a hassle, those who participate in the FBA program also get preferential treatment when it comes to search results as well as how their packages are shipped. Amazon power users who take advantage of the Amazon Prime membership option receive free 2-day shipping on countless products that Amazon sells directly, but also, on all of the items sold by those in the FBA program.

This means that by simply signing up for FBA you are already placing your future products at a huge advantage when compared to similar products that you will one day be competing against. The amount you are charging for shipping will also affect your Amazon rating in several ways, but suffice it to say, a lower shipping cost is always better. This, coupled with 2-day shipping, goes a long way towards creating positive mindshare, even if your product costs a little more, or is of a new private label brand that the customer has not yet heard of.

HOW IT WORKS

FBA works by allowing sellers to send their products directly to the nearest Amazon fulfilment facility where the products are then stored until they are sold. You then have the option of paying for additional preparation or labeling services as required while paying a monthly storage fee based on the amount of space your products require. Then, once a customer finds them online, Amazon takes care of all of the fulfilment tasks, including the all-important customer service and returns portion of the process which a more traditional dropshipping service would leave up to you.

It is important to understand just how valuable the fact that Amazon is fulfilling the orders in question is, especially when it comes to private label products from a new company. The Amazon name carries quite a bit of weight with customers, and having that name involved in the transaction will make them much more likely to go ahead and pull the trigger on the transaction in question. While they will hopefully become a loyal follower of your brand someday, being an FBA member gets you in the door. Studies show that FBA sellers typically see as much as a 30 percent boost in sales compared to more traditional sellers.

In return for the perks, FBA members pay a $40 monthly fee as well as a percentage of the sale price of each item. You will also be required to pay fees related to the weight of the item when it comes to shipping, any handling fees, pack or pick fees and storage fees based on the square footage. Additionally, you will be required to pay fees related to individually labeling all of your products as you will not want them commingled with other similar products as this will only dilute your brand. If you are unsure if this fee structure will fit the private label products, you may be hoping to one day sell you can check out the revenue calculator available on the official FBA site to determine if your idea is likely going to be a success.

When it comes to fleshing out your business plan it is important to factor in the benefits in terms of exposure that you will likely receive as well as any costs you might incur. This is especially true if you are going to be creating your own product line as you are going to need all of the potential customers you can get. If your initial idea does not appear as though it is going to work with FBA, you may want to consider alternative types of products as the solution is out there, you just have to do the work and find it.

A private label brand is any brand that it is not owned by a major company or organization. Over the past 20 years, private label brands have seen nearly double the growth of more mainstream brands, and the growth in niche markets where the importance of individual ingredient lists is much higher; much like customer interest levels when it comes to getting to know the creators of unique brands.

This is in large part due to the greater amount of perceived control that goes along with these types of products and it is something you can use to your advantage if marketed properly. What's more, when you decide to create your own private label you will have complete control over the branding and marketing of the product in question, allowing you to create something truly special that speaks directly to your target audience. Additionally, you will have the added advantage of perceived value as you don't have to deal with all of the added waste that comes from working with a major brand.

THE PRODUCT

For me personally, this is the most difficult part of starting a business. The beginning. The foundation, perhaps. Knowing what to sell to people is like knowing the exact shirt and tie combination to wear for a specific job interview. A polished cover letter and rehearsed answers for the interviewer's questions are far less effective if you dress inappropriately. Too casual is disrespectful and too formal makes you look desperate.

The items you choose to sell to people say something about you. Regardless of whether or not you have any practical use for the product, your signature will be all over them (sometimes literally). The material quality, the packaging, the storage conditions, the handling. While a one-time customer may not notice a lot of those things, a regular customer will likely be looking at all of those things and more.

CHOOSING A PRODUCT: If you did not start your business with a creative idea of your own already in mind then you will need to look for an opportunity. Any of the following is a great place to start

- Opportunities in Keywords

- Building an Interesting Brand

- Identify and Solve a Pain Point

- Identify and Cater to Passions

- Look for an Opportunity Gap

- Utilize Your Own Experience

- Capitalize on Trends

- Opportunities in Keywords

KEYWORDS: Starting from the top, we have opportunities derived from search engine keywords. Keywords are the words and phrases that users type into a search engine. Knowing a little bit about search engine optimization (SEO) is essential if you want to be competitive online. A lot of business owners are willing to handsomely pay savvy individuals to manage their advertising campaigns.

Anyway, the idea here is to find keywords that have a high search volume (a lot of people looking for it) and low competition (few good matches). That right there is a golden opportunity. Giving the people something that they already want means you can launch with a smaller ad campaign than if you were trying to get into a competitive market.

BUILDING AN INTERESTING BRAND: A popular strategy for entering a saturated and/or competitive market, as the 'new kid on the block' you have less money, less influence, and less experience than the older boys. Trying to keep up with them is an almost futile act. You need something unique. Something that only you have that makes others pay attention to you even if you are a rookie in a room full of champions and veterans. This is your brand.

I could list some specific examples but there are just so many! I suppose one of the most well-known is Apple's more stylish branding being used to separate their products from Microsoft's dull ones. Even a Goliath like Microsoft is not safe from an opponent who knows how to stand out from the rest.

You can take the same route as Apple and distinguish your brand visually. You could also just tell your own story. Few consumers think about the people behind brands like Wal-

Mart or McDonald's. Instead, they think of how huge those businesses are and how rich the owners and executives must be. Highlighting your status as a small business without a lot of capital can make you far more relatable to the average shopper.

<u>IDENTIFY AND SOLVE A PAIN POINT:</u> There has never been a better time to be alive in history. The best and brightest of us have worked diligently to make every one of us live comfortably. Once deadly diseases are now treatable if not curable. Modern vehicles make travel so easy that plans are being made to explore the solar system. Advancing technology continues to make performing tasks so easy that people are afraid of not having jobs in the near future.

All of the things that cause discomfort are pain points. I mentioned some big ones but there are small ones, too. I can type out this book on a computer because dipping pens in ink that smudged all over the paper was a pain point for writers. The printing press and typewriters were revolutionary even though they were not cures for cancer. Try isolating some minor frustrations and then think of products that can remove them.

Note that when I brought up advancing technology I also included a fear that people have. The solution to what was once a problem can create a new problem. Be on the lookout for innovations that change the way a lot of us live. Those changes can create an environment for a new pain point to develop.

<u>IDENTIFY AND CATER TO PASSIONS:</u> I think this type of opportunity is the easiest to understand. You identify something that a lot of people are interested and provide an additional something that appeals to those people. This is what many people do with blogs and vlogs to start building a following. Someone who wants to travel but is unable to will settle for a virtual escape in the meantime.

Fan merchandise falls under this category, too. You should get permission before reproducing symbols and logos that belong to someone else, but fan art can be sold legally as of the time that I am writing this. If you are an artist, slap that art onto clothes, mugs, and bags if you think the fanatics will buy them.

Not an artist? Well somebody has to supply all the clothes, mugs, and bags to be printed over. Creative types are all about that passion and you can take advantage of that. It is also possible that one person can do all of the above. If you share the same passion as your clients then a lot of this work could feel more like an addictive hobby. Cater responsibly.

<u>LOOK FOR AN OPPORTUNITY GAP:</u> As smartphones became ubiquitous in the early 2000s, the people ran into a problem. They wanted to take photos of themselves using their phones. However, it was near impossible to get the right angle and lighting while holding the device only an arm's length away. Friendly bystanders were a godsend but could not be relied

upon at all times. The people cried out for a solution and the market answered their cries with the Selfie Stick.

That is how you take advantage of an opportunity gap. Human beings always want 'more' regardless of how much they already have. People in houses want bigger houses. People who own a car want another car. People who get food delivered to their homes want faster delivery. There will always be a demand for something new to make living just a little bit easier. Provide something to achieve that goal and you will have plenty of business.

Opportunity gaps are like minor pain points; nobody complains because they are more of an inconvenience than a cause of stress. Discovering one will take research and awareness. You can ask the people around you about the products they use and if they feel like something is missing when they use them.

UTILIZE YOUR OWN EXPERIENCE: Young entrepreneurs are still young people. They are optimistic and ambitious with little to lose and so much to gain. Older people tend to move with caution and lower expectations. One of your biggest assets, as you age, is your experience. Wisdom cannot be bought or stolen and its value is priceless.

The more work experience and expertise you have in a field, the more of an advantage you have others who are entering it. Writing and publishing your own book should not only generate some income but also show others in the field that you know what you are talking about. As a consequence of that, any products you sell in the future will stand out because of your reputation.

Your choice of media does not have to be in writing. You can make videos or host seminars. The objective is just to make it known that you are an authority in your field. Not feeling confident? Do it regardless! If even one of your industry insights is unique it might be enough to establish a following.

CAPITALIZE ON TRENDS: This one is tricky. The idea is similar to that of finding opportunities in keywords. A trend has to be identified early and capitalized on immediately for the best results. Being the second person to catch on might not be good enough depending on consumer demand and how long the trend lasts.

Let us pretend that I have identified what I believe to be a trend. How do I confirm this? The most straightforward way is to buy a small amount of whatever I think I need to sell and put it up for sale.

If sales are anything less than stellar then either I am too late or I have not identified a trend at all. If it really is trendy I should see a significant amount of that product sold in a couple of days. The next step is to buy a lot more of that trendy product and make sure consumers know what I have done so.

<u>TIP:</u> I would like you to take a moment and reflect on your mindset. It is the one thing that will keep you going. Set it right, and no obstacle will deter you from that handsome Amazon deposit in your bank account.

Thanks to this online business, I was able to quit my day job and work for myself. Eventually, I reached a net profit level in the six-figure range and I stabilized there. I can give you all the details of my success in *"Amazon FBA Mastery Coaching: The Definitive Guide to Learn the Secret Way to Sell Fulfillment By Amazon"* which is available at Amazon.com

CHAPTER 14
DROPSHIPPING

When it comes to earning money, people look at various business models. If you want to do something but still keep your regular job, you have a few options. Dropshipping is a process that is recommended by several websites. The problem with drop shipping is the number of responsibilities that it involves. Unlike affiliate marketing where you promote a product for a business and hold no responsibility whatsoever for the quality of the product delivered, drop shipping holds you responsible for a faulty or bad quality product. You always need to be available to customers and provide them with support and assistance. Also, you need to go back and forth with the merchant and your buyer, which takes a lot of time. In its true sense, affiliate marketing is passive income, because once you create your blog page and promote it on your end, all you need to do is sit back and relax while customers continue shopping through your affiliate network.

It may take you a while to establish a strong blog and generate traffic to it but once this is done, you will automatically have people coming to your website or blog and going through your network to buy products.

CHAPTER 15
YOUTUBE VIDEOS

In addition to Facebook and Instagram, YouTube marketing has also gained a lot of popularity. There are various businesses that prefer to share videos in order to enhance marketing efforts, and the best way to share these videos is by sharing them on YouTube. The reason YouTube marketing is more effective when it comes to videos is that you can rest assured someone has watched your video when it's placed at the start as opposed to when the ad is placed in between a video that they are watching. YouTube is responsible for creating a lot of awareness for various businesses, and it also is effective when you are a startup. If you have little or no credibility, and you want to create mass awareness in a short time span, YouTube is probably your best bet.

As all of us know, YouTube belongs to Google – a company that has taken up most of the market today. With over a billion registered subscribers, people spend hours on YouTube each day watching videos across various genres. No matter what kind of videos you are looking for, you are sure to find them on YouTube. This gives you the leverage to add your advertisement to videos that are related to your business in some way or the other. When it comes to behavioral targeting, it is very effective to do it when you are doing it through YouTube. This is because you will find videos of all genres here and you will be able to relate your business to one of these genres.

YOUTUBE MARKETING STRATEGIES

Promoting your business on YouTube is great, but like all social media platforms, you need to begin with a strategy in mind. Without a strong strategy, your efforts on YouTube will go down the drain. There are various goals people have when they advertise on YouTube, and it depends on the nature of your business. If you are a personality or a public figure, the only reason you'll advertise on YouTube is to get more visibility, if you are a business and you want people to come to visit your website, then that needs to be your goal. There are also e-Commerce websites that would like to sell products, and these videos could simply include a 'buy now' link that directs a potential customer straight to their sales page to help increase sales. Your strategy needs to be based on your end goal and why you are advertising on YouTube in the first place.

CHAPTER 16
SOCIAL MEDIA INFLUENCER

The first question that you really need to ask yourself when you're laying down the foundation for your personal brand is whether you're capable of becoming an influencer in your own niche or not. For one to be able to influence people from a specific industry or niche, the influencer needs to have a tremendous amount of knowledge and information about the product or industry in general. Followers and fans should be so impressed by the profound knowledge of the influencer that they can directly have an impact on them and influence their thought processes. A person who is capable of being an influencer in their own niche is sort of like the expert of the industry. They should be able to provide proper guidance to his followers and fans. As an industry expert, they will share their experiences on all possible platforms, including articles, videos, social media, books, conferences, personal interactions, pamphlets, interviews, and so on.

DO YOU HAVE THE CAPABILITIES TO PROMOTE YOUR OWN PRODUCTS?

Not every manufacturer goes out on the market to promote his or her own products. There are some individuals who have the potential and power to market and promote their own products, while there are others who don't. You need to find out for yourself whether you have the right tools to influence people to invest in the products that you have to offer. Try to promote your products yourself a few times, and if you see a rise in sales and general inquiries for the product, you might just be the influencer that your company needs. If you see no increase in sales or maybe even a drop-in sales, maybe you should leave the promotion and branding to the professionals.

206 | THE HOLY GRAIL OF FINANCIAL FREEDOM

CHAPTER 17
EMAIL MARKETING
A POWERFUL LEAD GENERATION TOOL!

Another strategy that I see that not all bloggers are exploring is email marketing. For this to work to its fullest, it is essential that you have a list of correctly obtained emails, which is to let your own readers subscribe to your blogs or websites.

Many may think that Email Marketing does not have the same conversion strength as blog banners, but what I can say over the course of time exploring this type of advertising is that it converts more than the banners people insert in their blogs. Of course, for the success of these campaigns, it is necessary to respect the ethical limits of sending emails, not making our readers end up unsubscribing from your mailing list.

INCENTIVES AND SOCIAL NETWORKS

This is another subject that I think is very little explored by bloggers and webmasters. Social networks are places that move almost all people who access the internet, making the possibilities of generating leads very large if well explored. Also, the people who will see your campaigns on social networks are your friends or acquaintances, who know your reputation and what makes your reporting power great. Of course, to get feedback from this type of disclosure, you need to have a well-connected and influential profile on social networks.

UNDERSTAND THE MOST PROFITABLE REGIONS OF YOUR BLOG OR WEBSITE

Following the concept of working lead generation campaigns with recommendations within articles, there are also the articles that people publish that are specific about a particular product or service. This has a high conversion power, but one cannot abuse this and make their blogs strictly "commercial." In this case, it is important to understand the most viewed sites in our blogs.

I would suggest dividing your articles into 3 blogs, where the first block consists of the first paragraphs with an introduction about what will be treated, the second is composed by the middle of the article and the third by the final part of the article. With this, you can clearly say that the links that have the highest chance of conversion are those that are in the FINAL of the first block.

CHAPTER 18
COUPON WEBSITE

One of the easiest ways to increase your income today is through discount websites. These discount websites offer coupons that can be turned into income by anyone who knows how to use them. Since making money online is becoming harder nowadays due to the huge competition in all niche markets, knowing how to make money from discount coupons is a great opportunity.

Today, coupons have proven to be one of the easiest ways to make money online, and especially nowadays, that niche is still low in competitiveness. You can quickly create a discount coupon site even if you do not know about programming or design.

Discount coupon sites allow your users to receive discount coupons for multiple online stores. Users can use these discount codes to redeem unique and specific prices for that online store. So there are many online search prospects for "Discount Coupon." If you provide discount coupons to visitors to your online space, they will always receive the discounts available. People use these coupons to get a specific discount at that online store for wanted products, which always takes them back to their space. Once they complete your purchase online on your site, you will receive credit for this sale, and this store will send you your commission on your payment schedule.

Whenever you use a coupon or offer a link, the coupon sites earn a percentage on the purchase. This amount is paid by affiliate networks such as Lomadee, Zanox and Afilio. To register on these platforms is free, just have a website or blog to enable registration. The platforms have direct partnerships with the major retail networks and share the earnings of the sales indication with the affiliates who generated the nomination. Coupon sites use the links provided by these affiliate networks that have code that identifies the site.

These commissions vary according to the type of business. Example, in airfare usually is 1 to 2% in electronics on average 4% and so on. Each product type has a different margin. The harder the generation of business, the higher the commission.

If you are ready to start your own website and earn money with a discount coupon, you need the following items ready before you start increasing your income:

1. Register your domain name and host

2. Register name from the domain to your virtual space is the first step to start working to make money with coupons.

3. Apply as an affiliate

4. Install your coupon and theme plugin

Now your discount website is ready to be marketed. You will need to bring visitors to it, and there are innumerable ways to do it.

Write high-quality articles on "How to get a discount for a specific online store" and post those articles in some article directory with a link back to your discount coupon site. Join online forums where your audience is present. Help them get discounts on their desired online store with the forum posts. Create small but appealing videos on topics like "How to get discounts on wallmart.com?" And upload your video on YouTube by inserting your site link at the top of your video description.

With the above tips, making money from discount coupon websites has never been so easy, making you get the best for your income at the end of the month!

SECTION

TWO

LEARNING PROPERTY BASED METHODS TO EARN PASSIVE INCOME

CHAPTER 19
REAL ESTATE INVESTOR

This is one of the ancient and most well-known ways to generate passive income. The question remains on similar lines here too - How to make money in the real estate market?

As all of us know, there are two ways to make money from real estate:

1. Buy a property as an investment medium and then sell it, pocketing profits.

2. Owning and thus being able to secure a rent income.

Both alternatives look good, do not they? But what if you had a third option? One that would possibly make you profit much more than the previous ones, through expressive returns. Many people do not know what it really takes to make good gains. With the lack of good recommendations of truth, they end up being limited to the common - to buy or rent.

This alternative to buying or renting is precisely having a portfolio of Real Estate Funds. The mechanism is quite simple. You "buy" a part of a property and receive a rent corresponding to that part. For the sake of discussion in this and the following paragraphs, Countries are experiencing a downturn in the real estate market. And, buying low can mean big fortunes in the future. We are at the height of the rebates in a market that had long since stagnated. The timing is ideal and can boost various ways of investing. It's okay for you to be adept at buying or renting a classic. But in exact moments like this, you need to know the different possibilities to become a better investor of your money. And most importantly: invest safely.

Such guides and research videos and content can be found on almost every market, which again emphasizes the point that you may not have prior knowledge of this sector, but you can surely earn great returns if you invest wisely and safely.

As previously said, I started my entrepreneurial career online with a business called Amazon FBA and my life has completely changed in just twelve short months.

Thanks to this online business, I was able to quit my day job and work for myself.

But while I was more than pleased with my success, I realized that I needed to differentiate my business in order to continue to grow my financial security the way I wanted to. This is a fundamental requirement for continued growth and development. I needed another source of passive income because economic stability depends on having multiple sources of income.

After researching several opportunities, I knew that real estate investing would give me the perfect opportunity to continue to grow my wealth. I soon learned that even though I already have a six-figure income, it would not be needed for me to invest in real estate. I found so many ways to begin my career with little or no money down.

You will find many options available in the real estate market—opportunities that will give you a regular source of income for years to come. With the proper tools and techniques, which I intend to give you, you will be able to enjoy the exact same kind of success that I am currently enjoying in my life. With this knowledge, the only other thing you will need is to have a positive mindset and be prepared to succeed. This book is about the correct way to buy and maintain rental real estate properties. There is the right way and the wrong way to do it, just like any other field. I want to show you the right way to make money in this field. You can't just find a listing and assume it will be perfect. But there are ways to find good listings and this book will show you how to do it. This book will show you what a good rental property is, how to find it, and how to get it. And yes, there are ways to acquire property even if you don't have down payment money available or if you already have multiple mortgages on the books. Anything is possible. I will show you through my experiences how to be successful in the rental real estate market.

Successful real estate investing will give you everything you need to achieve present and future financial security. You will learn the basic of the business and what you need to know to grow your own empire and enjoy the same success that I am currently enjoying. You will learn how to overcome challenges and be able to anticipate issues that you can easily avoid on your path to success.

There are many reasons someone might choose this field as one in which they can make money—now and in the future. One of the most important reasons, at least in the beginning, is that you can start with one rental property while you continue to work at your regular job. Because let's be honest; most people can't just quit their day job the moment they buy their first rental property. Getting into the market this way will mean that you will need to work nights and weekends on the rental property but if it is a necessary way to get started, then that is what you will do. Once you have several properties and you are enjoying regular cash flow then you might be able to drop down to part-time or to quit altogether. Be patient; it will happen.

The real estate market is relatively easy to learn and that includes rental property investing. There are many available resources, both in the library and online, that will give you the answer to any question you might have. There are many people who are more than willing to share the things they have learned with those who are just starting out.

Buying rental property allows you to manage your monetary investment directly if you chose to. Some people will hire a property manager but if this is your full-time job and you want to be a hands-on kind of landlord, this is the business to do it in. And if you enjoy being in charge and controlling events, then rental property is the market for you because you are responsible directly for what happens to your investment. It is your responsibility to check out the property before you buy it to make sure it is a good investment. It is your job to make certain the property is suitable for and attractive to potential renters. The preferred way for many people to do this is to manage the business themselves.

Of all the things that people can give up in life, people will always need somewhere to live. Not everyone can afford to become a homeowner because even if they have the down payment they may not have the income to be able to afford the regular upkeep of a house. Not everyone wants to be a homeowner. For whatever reason you can think of, there will always be people who need to rent somewhere to live. And you can provide this place.

Rental property is real; it is a tangible investment. You can see it right in front of you. If you make an improvement on the property, then you can see how much better it looks afterward. Rental property may occasionally drop in value but it will always come back up and while it is rented to someone you will continue to make money. And you can use other people's money to grow your investments. Other people will help with down payments. Other people will pay you rent money to live in your house.

And along with the nearly constant cash flow, you will also enjoy tax breaks as the owner of rental property. There are many tax laws that make a favorable environment for property owners. For instance, the interest expense that you pay along with your monthly mortgage payment is tax deductible. Your operating expenses are also deductible. This means that your depreciation, insurance, property taxes, and operating expenses are all deductible. This is an extra layer of savings that will be much enjoyed at tax time.

Buying real estate to use as rental property is a fantastic investment if you are willing to do what you need to do to be successful. You will get amazing returns if you just learn the processes. The best thing about rental property is that they become better investments the longer that you own them. You make cash flow from rental properties every month, money that comes to you on a regular basis. Your cash flow will naturally increase over time because the rate of rental payments will increase but your mortgage payment will remain steady, thus making your cash flow increase on a regular basis. When the mortgage is paid off the cash flow will significantly increase.

And by purchasing rental property you are building equity for your future, including money for your retirement. The monetary difference between what you owe and what the house is worth is the equity. Since the value of the property will increase over time as the amount that you owe becomes less, your equity is always increasing. And once the properties are paid off, the rental income will provide a nice regular source of income for your later years.

Investing in rental property has many overall benefits and will prove to be a great source for passive income. Your potential for profit will increase because the value of rental property increases with the increasing demand for property. There are several important advantages to investing in real estate for rental property. As long as you go into this with your eyes wide open and a ready mindset, you will be successful.

Investors are able to find rental properties that are available for sale by using many different techniques. If you rely on a wide variety of resources to help you find properties, then you will be giving yourself the best overall possible chance to find the investment property that is perfect for you.

Networking is one way that many people use to find rental properties. This method will give you access to properties that the general public may not know about yet. People are often hearing about their friends and neighbors who are thinking about selling their homes. This could give you the inside track on a new property to purchase. Professional contacts such as attorneys or contractors might also have information regarding other properties for sale.

Some people prefer to join investment clubs that are groups of people who spend their time looking for and talking about real estate. These clubs may have a small annual membership fee of a few hundred dollars but that can be well worth it for the chance to find new properties to buy. And the membership fee is most likely tax deductible as a business expense. You might also belong to a group of other property investors or landlords who will hear about available properties that they themselves might not be interested in.

Realtors are a great source of information regarding properties to buy for rental properties. After all, the realtor's job is to locate properties for sale for people who want to buy them and to locate people to buy the properties their clients want to sell. You can easily make an appointment with a realtor to look at individual listings. Or you can drive through a particular area that you might want to own property in to see if any properties are for sale. If you find any, you can call the realtor listed on the sign and make an appointment to see the house. You can also check out open houses where you can actually go through the house and look at it with less intimate contact with the realtor since hopefully many people will be viewing the house at the same time you are.

Banks often have a backlog of properties available that are for sale because they have been foreclosed on. Banks like to sell these properties because they do not bring in any income for the bank sitting empty and unused. These properties are generally listed with a realtor eventually but if you can catch a listing before it goes to the realtor then you can avoid paying the realtor's fees and this will save you money.

Do not overlook the newspaper as a valuable source of information. Many people get their news online these days but there are certain things that will still be found in the newspaper in black and white print. In the classified section you will find notices of foreclosures or sheriff's sales. A foreclosure sale is held when a lending institution has reacquired a property from an owner who could not or did not make their monthly mortgage payment. The lender will take allow all interested people to tour the property and then they will take bids for buying the property, either during a live auction or by sealed bid. The bidder with the best bid wins. These properties are generally sold for the value of the note owing on the house so it is possible to pick up a good property for less money. These are sometimes referred to as sheriff's sales. These will be listed in the newspaper because they must be publicly announced.

Buying property at a foreclosure sale or a sheriff's sale is a great way to find a good deal on a property for investment purposes. These are local sales held by the county government. These sales are open to the public. Anyone who wants to bid on a property must have the funds in place prior to the sale and you must have proof that the funds are available. Property listings, either online or in the newspaper, will include the address and description of the property and the listing will also include the upset price. This is the minimum amount that the plaintiff (the one who is selling the property) will take as a bid for the property. It is a good idea to do a complete coverage title search on any property you might want to buy. Searching the title for discrepancies will tell you if there are any liens against the house, such as contractor liens, utility company liens, or even liens from any source that collects tax money. Liens are lawsuits placed on a property when that particular bill has not been paid by the homeowner. So if you hire someone to put new gutters on your house and you never pay him, he can file a lien against your property. These liens may or may not be satisfied (paid off) by the proceeds from the sale. If they are not, then the new owner is responsible for paying them.

The amount of money that you bid on a property depends on two things: how much is the minimum required bid and how much are you willing to spend. You must bring a certified check, also known as a cashier's check or an official check, for the down payment. You will need to know what percentage of the purchase price the down payment must be. It might be ten percent, fifteen percent, or twenty percent. So if you are willing to pay at the most $200,000 for the property then you must bring a check for twenty thousand dollars on a ten percent down, thirty thousand dollars on a fifteen percent down, and forty thousand dollars on a twenty percent down. Closing depends on the term of the local county sheriff's office but it is usually within thirty days. That means in thirty days from the auction you must have your financing arranged and have taken possession of the house.

When you are ready to buy your first property you need to decide what your personal criteria will be for the property. Making this list is like making a shopping list for the grocery store. Deciding before your search exactly what you are looking for will help keep you focused on the search so that you will be able to find the kind of properties that you are looking for. When you are making your list be sure to think about all of the attributes you would like a house to have. If you are in a large city and looking in the suburbs, which city would you prefer? Which neighborhood would you like to buy into? How big will the lot be and how many square feet will be in the house. Do you want to buy move-in ready or a fixer-upper? What is the CAP rate? How much cash flow can you expect to receive? What is the potential for appreciation?

CAP rate refers to the term capitalization rate, which is the amount of money you would expect to receive from a property over the period of one year. It will help you to determine whether or not a particular property is a good investment. The CAP rate is the ratio of property asset value to net operating income. So let's say you are looking at two different properties that are already set up as rental units. Both properties are rented for ninety-five percent of the year.

Property A	Property B
Value $500,000	Value $600,000
Occupancy rate 95%	Occupancy rate 95%
Gross rental income $60,000	Gross rental income $72,000
Operating expenses $25,000	Operating expenses $32,000

The first step in the equation is to multiply the gross rental income by the occupancy rate:

Property A: 95% x $60,000 = $57,000
Property B: 95% x $72,000 = $68,400

The next step is to subtract the operating expenses:

Property A: $57,000 - $25,000 = $32,000
Property B: $68,400 - $32,000 = $36,400

Now you have the Net Operating Income (NOI). This is the yearly income that is generated by a rental property counting all of the income that is generated from operations and subtracting the expenses that come from operating the property. Divide the NOI number by the current value of the property to get the CAP rate:

Property A: $32,000/$500,000 = 0.064
Property B: $36,400/$600,000 = 0.060

Since the CAP rate is always expressed as a percentage, now multiply each number by one hundred:

Property A: 0.064 x 100 = 6.4% CAP rate

Property B: 0.060 x 100 = 6% CAP rate

These two properties have a similar CAP rate. The determining factor in this example would be some other consideration, such as sales price or location. The figures for the operating expenses, rental income, and occupancy rate can be obtained from the realtor.

An acceptable CAP rate falls somewhere between four percent and ten percent. The CAP rate should just be used as an indicator of profitability while considering other factors. Obviously if the CAP rate falls out of these percentages then the property might not make you the money you desire. You also need to consider local demand, inventory that is available in the area, and the type of property this one is specifically. As an example, a CAP rate of four percent might be quite normal in areas of high demand such as New York City and California. But in an area where the demand is lower, such as an area that is going through regeneration or in a rural area, the normal CAP rate might be ten percent or even higher.

Most buyers look for a higher CAP rate, which means the price to purchase the property is rather low when compared to the net operating income. Unfortunately, a lower CAP rate usually represents a lower risk property where a higher CAP rate usually means a property with a higher risk. A property that has a higher CAP rate might be located in an area that doesn't have much opportunity for regular rental increases or where property does not appreciate as well as it does in other areas. As an investor you will need to weigh all of these factors when deciding on a property to purchase.

One thing to remember when comparing CAP rates is to compare rates on similar properties. This just means to compare properties that are similar to each other and are in similar areas. An investment property that is a multifamily rental unit will probably have a CAP rate that is much lower than a commercial building that is full of retail tenants. This means that the multifamily unit will probably be an investment of lower reward than the commercial building but it will also probably be a lower risk. This is because in times of economic downturn people still need to live somewhere, where retail customers might close up and move away.

CAP rates are affected by four factors:

2.1 INTEREST RATES: Property values typically fall when interest rates rise. When the rates rise, the debt ratio usually rises which will mean a decrease in net cash flow so lower CAP rates come from rising interest rates. The rent will remain the same but if the interest rate is higher then you will not make as large of a profit.

2.2 AVAILABLE INVENTORY: This term refers to the number of properties that are available in one particular area. If the inventory is lower the demand for property will be higher, this will lead to properties with a lower CAP rate.

2.3 ASSET CLASS: This is the factor that tells what type of property it is, like a commercial property, a single-family dwelling, an apartment building, etc. Residential properties usually have lower CAP rates than commercial properties because you can charge a higher rent to a commercial tenant.

2.4 LOCATION: The local economy and property demand is driven by the location of the property. A property in a more desirable location will have a higher value and higher rents, which will affect the overall CAP rate.

CAP rate is only one way to evaluate properties when deciding which property is the better investment. You should really be prepared to consider several factors when deciding which property will be the best investment property for you to buy. Doing this will give you a better, more well-rounded picture of the property and whether it has a reasonable potential to be a good investment for you. Particularly if the property needs to be remodeled or is vacant you will probably want to use extra tools in order to evaluate it. Here are several ways to make an evaluation of a potential investment property:

2.4.1 RETURN ON INVESTMENT (ROI): Usually ten percent or more is considered to be a good ROI for any real estate investment property. ROI is determined by dividing your total investment into your annual return. Annual return is determined by subtracting the amount of expenses from the total rental income.

2.4.2 THE PERCENTAGE RULE: This is the one percent rule or the two percent rule, both are used equally. This guide says that the monthly gross income should be at least one percent, or two percent, of the price of the purchase. If the monthly gross income is more than one percent of the price of the purchase, then the property usually will have a positive flow of cash.

2.4.3 GROSS RENTAL YIELD: Take the collected annual rent by the total cost of the property and then multiply by one hundred; the higher the number the better the yield. The total cost of the property will include any renovation costs, closing costs, and the purchase price.

2.4.4 CASH FLOW: See if the expected monthly rental income covers the monthly costs that will include the homeowner's association fees, utilities, taxes, insurance, and mortgage payment. If the rental amount collected exceeds the amount of expenses, then the cash flow is positive.

2.4.5 PER-UNIT PRICE: In a multifamily unit or a commercial building take the purchase price and divide it by the number of units in the building. This will give you a price per unit so that you can determine if the unit is worth that price based on its cosmetic appearance and overall usefulness.

<u>2.4.6 COMPARABLE PROPERTIES</u>: Get the figures from the last three to six months of the sale price, rental rates, and occupancy rates for buildings that are similar to the building you are considering purchasing. When comparing properties, they need to be similar in size, have amenities that are similar, and be the same types of properties.

When considering the other factors that are listed on your particular list of criteria, remember that you have the right to be as demanding as you want to be. No one can tell you what your particular investment should look like. Just remember that if you are too narrow in your consideration, you might not have very much inventory to choose from. But when you are able to specify the particular criteria of the rental property, you want to own it will be easy for you to search for a property to buy. And in knowing what you want to buy you will be better able to tell other people what you are looking for. Just telling people "Hey, I'm looking for rental properties to buy" will probably get you a nice smile. But telling people "Hey, I'm looking for a three-bedroom, two bath, single family home on a one-acre lot in the Millwood are of town" will probably get you some action on your request.

The most important part of the package of criteria that you will assemble is the financial part of your package. If the financial component of the deal does not add up to a profit, that property will probably not be a good deal. Usually a real estate listing will not tell you the information that you might find important to know about the financial information of a property. While you might be able to calculate an estimation for the amount of rental income a property might bring in, you will not immediately know how much cash flow the property brings in every month, if the property is overpriced, or exactly how much you should offer on the property. And even though you might love working a spreadsheet, it will not make sense to work one up for each property you are looking at. This is when you learn to use the "rules."

The 'rules' comes from the term "rules of thumb." These rules will give a buyer a rapid way to evaluate the financial health of a property. Using these rules is not exact and should not be the only consideration used to determine the worth of a property. These rules can help you quickly decide if a property may or may not be worth pursuing.

We have already discussed the one percent or two percent, rule. This rule is that whichever percent you use the monthly rental income should be that percentage of the purchase price. So using this rule a house that is priced at $100,000 should bring either $1000 or $2000 in rent each month. This is a very simple way to compare properties but it can let you know whether or not a particular property needs more investigation. Using the rule from the other way works like this: if the monthly rent is $500, you would not pay more than $50,000 for the house at the rate of one percent.

Then there is the fifty percent rule. This rule will help you to somewhat accurately tell how much your monthly expenses will be on the property. This rule is that fifty percent of your monthly income will be used for expenses on the property and this does not include the monthly mortgage payment. Since most real estate listings will tell you how much monthly income comes from the property you can easily get a good estimate of your monthly cash flow. Take the monthly income and divide that number in half. So half will go to expense and the other half needs to be enough to cover the mortgage. Anything left over is cash flow. The fifty percent for expenses will need to cover rehab costs for tenant turnover, management costs, utilities, vacancies, taxes, insurance, repairs, and some savings for the larger cost items like repaving or a new roof.

The last rule that is often used is the seventy percent rule. This rule is used by investors to determine quickly the maximum amount of the purchase price that you should offer. This number is based on the after-repair value (ARV) of the property and is used for those properties that will require a major renovation before they are ready to rent. This rule says you should pay no more than seventy percent of the value of the property after repairs minus the costs of the repairs. Use the following as an example:

This property needs extensive repair before it can be rented. After renovation it should sell for about two hundred thousand dollars. It needs around thirty-five thousand dollars in repair work. So to use the seventy percent rule you would multiply two hundred thousand by seventy percent to get one hundred forty thousand and then subtract the thirty-five thousand for the repair costs. That means the most you should pay for this property would be one hundred five thousand dollars.

Keep in mind that the rules of them are only used to give an efficient and quick way to screen a property. Any property that falls far out of line of one of the rules is probably not worth investing any more time or attention and especially not money.

When you are ready to buy a property, you will certainly not hand over a check and get keys in return. It does not work as quickly as it seems to work on television. There is a set process that is followed every time you purchase a property, no matter what type of property it is.

So let's begin at the point where you have found the property you want and you are ready to buy it. Your very first step is to decide how you are going to finance this purchase. This just means that you already have in mind a definite idea of how you are going to pay for this property. You need to be pre-approved by the lender if you are going to use a loan from any financial institution. If you have the funds and want to do an all cash offer, then those funds need to be liquid and available immediately. Liquid means they are sitting in a bank account or a credit union account and you can walk in the door and get an official check for the amount you need. If you are planning to use the proceeds from the sale of the jewelry Aunt Martha left you in her will, then that jewelry needs to have been already sold and the money put into an account. Money is liquid, property is an asset. Most real estate agents as well as anyone who has been buying real estate for any length of time, will recommend that you have your financing in place first before you ever go looking for property. If you find a great deal the chances are good that someone else found that same great deal, and whoever brings the money to the table first wins. So have your choice of financing ready.

Now you want you make an offer. This offer is made on paper, usually on a pre-printed form that has all of the correct legal terms on it. You will also determine the amount of time the offer will be good for. You and your real estate agent (if you are using one) will simply fill in the blanks and then it will go to the seller or their real estate agent. The seller's real estate agent will take it to their client and together they will discuss the offer and determine if it is acceptable to them. If you are not using an agent, you can find appropriate forms online but have your attorney look over the form before you submit it to make sure there are no errors.

When making an offer you do not need to offer the sale price. Perhaps the property needs renovation and the seventy percent rule calculations you did came up with a purchase price lower than what the seller is asking for. Sometimes sellers will ask for a price higher than what the property is worth to see how much they can get. It is perfectly acceptable to offer less than the sales price. Also in your offer you will put any contingencies that you have. These are stipulations that must occur before you will agree to buy the property. You may require any number of contingencies in the offer:

2.5 HOME INSPECTION: This will allow you to hire a home inspector who is certified by your state to do home inspections. While home inspectors can't possibly see all the problems a property might have, they can certainly see problems that might cause a hefty repair bill like the need for foundation work or a new work.

Be prepared to be excited and energized by what you will see in this book. This book will fill you with knowledge and excitement and everything you need to be successful in the rental property real estate market.

You will quickly learn how much I love the world of rental property real estate. Since I have discovered how easy it is to make money at this and how much fun it actually is I really don't want to stop. I originally got into this business as an addition to my portfolio. I was already enjoying success with my Amazon online business but I knew I needed to diversify if I wanted to keep growing my wealth and my future possibilities. So I chose real estate rental property.

I can give the all the details of my success in *"Rental Property Investing: Secrets of a Real Estate Building Empire"* which is available on Amazon.com.

CHAPTER 20
REAL ESTATE CROWDFUNDED

Buying to lease has seen a resurgence in recent times. For those who have the ability to borrow or already have enough capital, real estate investment for rent seems very attractive, especially when we compare it with greedy savings rates and shareholder market volatility. What also attracts in this investment is the recurrence of the revenues and the passive character, that is, you need to do little to receive your rents after the initial investment.

Here I must stop you once to draw your attention: beware of low-interest rates! They are volatile in nature and you must to do the math to see if you can afford to invest if the rates go up. However, to help you, I have mentioned some essential tips you can keep in mind to invest more successfully in the lease market (includes crowdfunded properties).

1. INVESTIGATE THE MARKET

If you are new to the real estate market, it is important that you become aware of the risks and opportunities. Make sure that buying for lease is the investment you are looking for. Your money may be able to perform better elsewhere. However, buying for lease means that you will have your capital tied up on a property that may lose value.

Investing in real estate involves committing hundreds of thousands of your currency to a property and usually requires a mortgage. When home prices rise, it is possible to make large leveraged gains on your home equity loan, but when your assets fall, they are hit, and the mortgage remains the same.

Investment in real estate has been extremely profitable for many people, both in terms of income and in terms of capital gains, but it is essential that you enter it with your eyes wide open, identifying the potential advantages and disadvantages. If you know someone who invested in leasing, ask him about his experience - the wrinkles he won, the hair he lost, everything ...

The more knowledge you have and the more research you do, the more likely your investment will be worth it.

2. CHOOSE AN ATTRACTIVE AREA

Attractive does not mean cheap or expensive. Attractive means a place where people would like to live, and this may be due to several reasons. What is the neighborhood in your city that has a special appeal? If you live in a suburban area, what are transports like? Where are good schools for young families? Where do the students want to live?

These neighborhoods have more appeal when it comes to guaranteeing income (especially for temporary rent), but if you look for absolute return (valuation of the property plus income), you may be looking for neighborhoods still in revitalization. In the end, you have to look at whether the property you can and want to buy is in a place where people would like to live. These questions may seem too simplistic, but they are probably the most important aspect of an investment for lease.

3. DO THE MATH

Before you go running to the computer to look at specialty sites for a home, sit down with a pen and paper and note the cost of the homes you are looking for and the income you want to get. Better yet, the first question you need to answer is: what is the fair value of a home? One of the most common mistakes for renters is to forget to incorporate expenses when calculating the cap rate or the valuation.

While it is normal to value the price of housing in the long term, experts say that they should invest to generate income, not for capital gains in the short term. In short, to compare the values of different properties, you must use the formula of the cap rate. For example, if a property has operating results of € 10,000 and the property value is € 200,000, then it has a cap rate of 5%.

That is if a house that costs € 300,000 generates a cap rate of 6% (if everything else is constant) it is a better investment to rent than the cheapest house (cap rate = 5%). The absolute value is your limit, but the important thing is to calculate what income you can get from the property versus the house price (relative value).

4. THE IMPORTANCE OF MANAGING EXPENDITURE

In this first part, we explained how to analyze the earning potential of real estate. Now let's talk about how the return potential affects the value of it. Let's talk about a concept which can work wonders for you in this market and in analyzing and calculating what your returns will be.

An important concept which helps a lot while investing and calculating returns in this sector is - multiples.

When a baker wants to trade his bakery, the tricky way to come up with a value would be to hire a specialist to project his cash flows, establish a discount rate that would be appropriate to the risk, and thus get a negotiation. This is not practical, and bakers prefer to take the easy way out. With many years of transactions, he has established a practice of trading bakeries based on multiples of annual sales.

So if you buy bakeries for your annual turnover or maybe, if it's a great quality bakery 1.3 times - and so on. What is important is that every experienced baker knows, more or less, how profitable a bakery is. Then it is implied that the business has the potential to generate a certain profit and therefore, in an indirect way, a projection is being defined cash flow and a discount rate.

Negotiation flows much more easily because billing is verifiable. Just count the money that is in the cash register every day for a month. The comparison is also easier since to know if a bakery is cheap or expensive, just observe the multiple required, starting with the reference at once the billing. In the same way that the baker sells his business based on a billing multiple, shopping center companies negotiate their business on a multiple basis.

In the case in question, the most widely used multiple is the capitalization rate (discussed above).

Cap rate = Operating Result / Property Value

The mergers and acquisitions market is always disclosing recent transactions, and all of them give us a good idea of the current cap rate.

CHAPTER 21
AIRPORT PARKING INVESTOR

OW TO ASSEMBLE A PARKING LOT AND MAKE MONEY WITH THE GAP
To set up a parking lot, business owners should consider the market for the deal. Investing in parking is a tempting business as parking lots keep pace with the growing demand for car space, a business opportunity that comes with increasing numbers of cars and other factors linked to insecurity and a greater number of stolen vehicle incidents. But, beware - Avoid Committing the First Trip Entrepreneurs ERROR!

The need for such types of product in the market is well established with the ever-increasing car space and the steady growth in the buying power and living standards of the people, globally. In addition, you can also see this on a personal front, when you leave your car parked on public roads, you run the risk of burglaries, car predation by passers-by, the car's paint is badly damaged for a long time in the sun, and it is quite uncomfortable to pick up a car on a rainy day. Therefore, parking expenses have become a necessity for those who need to get around with vehicles and keep their car safe.

By all the factors already mentioned above is that this business model has become one of the most profitable and is one of the most sought after. But there are a few things which you still need to keep in mind:

LOCATION TO BUILD A PARKING

It is important that the location of your future parking space is located where there are no vacancies available in the nearby streets, even more so that there are cities where vacancies are offered by the city hall with values well considered. Another tip is to choose a place that is very visible to customers, that everyone has easy access to.

The perfect location of a parking lot that works for workers and not just shoppers is to be close to offices and a lot of shopping outlets. Do a good search in your city and if possible, visit the traffic department to find out the ideal spot. It needs to be visible, have a good possibility of external maneuvering and away from bottled spots of local traffic.

It is important to hire a security company to monitor the vehicles; after all, you will be responsible if something happens. A parking lot may also be located in residential locations serving condominiums, which will be a great business opportunity for entrepreneurs. See also about digital entrepreneurship.

BUSINESS TIPS

To retain customers, parking can be located in condominiums, which may establish a contractual system in which residents can receive rent for, monthly or fortnightly. The business may also work in companies; to carry out the activities in this way, the parking lots must win contracts or bids to render their services in public or private companies. This system also represents a profitable niche market.

Advertising of a parking lot is important, and one of the most effective ways to publicize it is through pamphlets. So we can see that parking can work independently as a company with its own or rented premises, can be located in condominiums of houses and apartments, located in the underground of public or private companies or still operate in shopping centers.

SERVICES OFFERED

In a Non-Location Car Park and hiring system, parking facilities prevail for the quality of services offered. Know that competition is fierce, and only those parking lots that guarantee first-class service and safety will win contracts. One tip to attract customers is to offer car wash and jet labs.

One option for parking services may be those that are exclusive to events. This parking style requires more workforce training that can be hired according to demand, but qualified. These services are usually hired by the event organizer and will require valet service, security and fixed value services for the event.

In addition to the services mentioned above, there are also exclusive services for restaurants or nightclubs, which usually work through contracts between businessmen and nightclubs or restaurants.

STRUCTURE OF A PARKING

The infrastructure of a parking lot should be well-suited so that all your customers feel safe when they leave your car. The tip is to use a complete property or an already empty area in an urban center for purchase or rent. The structure must have an area of at least 1000 m² of covered area and automatic gates. Drop everything and build a good flat area. It will require a medium investment, but it will be a great differential of your enterprise.

In a parking lot they should have signaling devices, valets, demarcation of seats, light poles, guards with guards, ratchets for cards and an office. The floor can be covered with gravel, cement or asphalt, at your discretion. The idea is to have a cover to protect cars and customers from sun and rain. Without a doubt, parking must be automated to provide safety and greater agility in operations. The automation should serve to register customers and thus be able to work through identification cards, barcode readers, ATMs for ticketing and so on.

INVESTMENTS TO BUILD A PARKING

Such parking's require initial investments in facilities, and facility equipment required for production processes such as clock-to-date, lighting, security systems with alarms, electronic gates, furniture and office equipment, telephone and fax. The investments will also be with personnel, automation and computerization, besides the costs and administrative expenses required for the legalization of the company.

With this, the initial investment capital varies according to the size of the enterprise. This amount can be higher or lower, according to the area and value of the property for purchase or rent.

STAFF

The choice of staff to work in the parking lot should consider points such as the ability to serve, driver's license, responsibility and above all, honesty. The work team will be composed of boxes, valets, guards, attendants and administrator who may be the owner / businessman. Depending on the structure of the parking lot, this functional frame may be smaller.

STANDARDS FOR THE PARKING SECTOR

To set up a car park, the entrepreneur must consider that it is necessary to meet certain standards that are part of the legislation that protects the consumer, and also remember that consumers have information about these standards and know their rights.

An important, yet simple thing to remember is the price information that should be clearly visible. Other information that should be visible is the number of spots and whether there are valets.

Important reminder: all parking must have insurance against robbery or theft, according to the legislation of each state or municipality. Otherwise the vehicle would not be totally safe just because it is in the parking lot.

CHAPTER 22
ONLINE MARKET PLACE
AIRBNB

W HY IS AIRBNB SO SUCCESSFUL? AND WHAT ARE THE FACTORS YOU NEED TO KEEP IN MIND WHILE TRYING THIS OUT?
A lot of people believe that Airbnb started off as a streamlined app with multiple options to reserve hotel rooms, apartments or private rooms that they could rent when they were on vacation. The truth is that the Airbnb founders had their share of struggle, and it started off as something that was listed on Craigslist before they gained popularity. Today, Airbnb listings are no longer allowed on Craigslist, and the business itself has become a $30 billion business with services like no other. The fact that Airbnb manages to cater to the requirements of low budget travelers, as well as those looking for luxury accommodations, makes it accessible to all. The filters available on the platform enable people who love traveling to combine affordability with adventure, thereby making it extremely trendy.

There are a number of people who wonder why Airbnb is such a popular marketplace and what made it grow so tremendously in a short time span. Here we have a look at some of the main reasons why Airbnb is in demand and why it is showing no signs of slowing down any time soon.

IT IS A FREE MARKET!

One of the best things for Airbnb is that it's free to accept for both parties. Unlike most other platforms, users need to register, sign up, and pay a certain fee in order to list their properties on the website. Airbnb allows you to use its platform without charging you any money. If you are a skeptical host and you don't want to invest any money in your business plan, then advertising is one of the last things that should be on your mind.

IT IS AN OPEN PLATFORM

Airbnb has a streamlined platform which is efficient, and you can choose the kind of property that you want to rent out. Whether you have a single bedroom in your house, an entire apartment or you are a hotel owner who's looking to rent out your hotel room; you can still list your property on Airbnb. If you have free space and you are looking for the best way to utilize the space and begin earning money out of it, then you need Airbnb. The hosts on Airbnb have an easy and convenient way to monetize their space that was otherwise just an empty space.

AFFORDABLE

Airbnb gives travelers the option of choosing between really reasonable and affordable properties and luxurious multi-storied apartments that come with a Jacuzzi. This means people can now rent out their properties irrespective of what kind of property they want to list. If you had a financial crisis recently and you are looking for some way to earn money, you don't have to invest in a new property. All you need to do is clear up your spare bedroom, and you can make it Airbnb ready. This is a zero-investment business that you can start, and it can help you get on your feet. There are several families who register on Airbnb when they have financial problems. In fact, that is how the business idea was conceived. Airbnb listings can help people to cope with their financial problems effectively.

SOCIALIZING

One of the reasons people hate staying at a hotel is because it is not warm and welcoming, and you do not feel at home. When you have an Airbnb listing, you can provide people with that warm and homely feeling that they usually crave when they are away from home. The reason why Airbnb works so well is that you interact with the guests as much as they want to, and it helps them feel welcome in a new country, state, or city. Helping them feel welcome not only lowers anxiety levels, but it also gives them the confidence to explore the place a little more. Language isn't something that stops you from communicating with someone because there are amazing translators that are available on your smartphone that can help to communicate with people.

LOCATION

One of the best things about Airbnb is it allows people to search for location-specific apartments or places to rent out. This means that when someone looks for a place in your specific location, your listing will be one of the first listings that will show up. The fact that a person can narrow down their selection to every little detail, including the location and the amenities that are provided, makes it a lot easier for travelers to reserve an Airbnb room rather than look for a cheap hotel or motel. When it comes to choosing a place to rent out on a holiday, flexibility is something that people pay a lot of attention to and Airbnb hosts can be more flexible and understanding than most hotels. This makes it a preferred choice for travellers. It's also more comforting on various levels and this is why people seek that warmth and comfort in the homes they rent out. It is a simple model that works well for both parties.

CHAPTER 23
SHORT TERM LET

As an Airbnb host (or a short term let host. I will be using these terms interchangeably here), you are somebody who is not only earning a passive income, but you are also a business person. The minute you look at your hosting services as a business, that's when you will realize the importance of the quality of services that you provide. As an Airbnb host, you are also required to provide the right management solutions to the business plan that you have come up with. If you have experience in running a business you don't need to stress too much because with a little effort and the right decision, not only will you be able to run your Airbnb apartment like no other, but you will also make sure that you keep the guests as happy as possible. Here is a look at some interesting techniques for business management that comes in handy for an Airbnb host.

USE PROFESSIONAL CLEANING SERVICES

Airbnb hosts tend to try and save money by hiring people that are cheap labor to get the cleaning procedures done in the apartment on a regular basis. This is something you should not compromise on because it is vital that you keep your house sparkling clean throughout the year if you want your guests to stay happy. Spending a little extra money on professional cleaning services makes a lot of sense after every guest checks out in case you don't have a professional cleaner who works for you. Keep in mind that every little nook and corner of the house should be cleaned perfectly, and there should be nothing that is overlooked.

As we have discussed before, there should always be two sets of cleaning that you choose - one which is basic cleaning and the other which is advanced cleaning that needs to take place as soon as the guests leave the space. You should have a dedicated cleaning team working for you because in case one of the training people is sick, you always have a backup. As an Airbnb host, you always look to grow, and the best way to do this is to keep getting positive reviews from people in terms of the cleanliness and hygiene of your space.

OUTSOURCE AS MUCH AS POSSIBLE

Even if you have one house that you have rented out on Airbnb, it could get difficult for you to constantly look after the guests when you have a 9 to 5 job that you need to live up to. In this case, the best thing to do is to outsource most of the jobs to other people. When it comes to cleaning you should always have a dedicated team who will clean your apartment from time to time, who handles the supplies for the apartment on a regular basis, and you should always have someone who looks after the laundry. You will also need a caretaker; however, this is something you can consider later on when you have multiple locations to handle or when your bookings are constantly flowing in.

USE AN ACCOUNTING SOFTWARE

It is very easy for an Airbnb host to believe that they will manage to handle the accounts of the apartment without having to depend on any software to do the calculations for them. However, minor expenses can lead to something major, and you'll end up with no profit in hand unless you have a good accounting system in place. If you don't have one, you can always purchase one at a minimal fee so that you know what the rate you charged for the apartment is, including the taxes and there is a certain profit left even after all the other expenses have been considered. You need to make sure that you list every little detail in this account and it accounts for even a single egg that has been purchased.

SET ASIDE A BUDGET BEFORE YOU START

An Airbnb listing may be free, and you don't have to spend money in order to become an Airbnb host, however there are a number of expenses that come up when you decide to rent your property, and this may be very unexpected, so you need to have a certain amount of money that is set aside. Imagine the first time you rent out your property and the person destroys a few valuables. You could end up in a loss just like that in the business. If you want the show to go on, you must be able to deal with the shortcomings and overcome them as soon as possible.

Before you decide to sign up as an Airbnb host, make sure that you set aside some money that you label as emergency expenses. While this money may not be needed, it's always good to have it handy and it's better to stay prepared in advance. Even with every profit that comes in, you should take out a certain amount of money from it and keep it aside for emergency funds. Later, the same money should be used for additional expenses like renovation or minor repair work that is needed around the house. When you do this, you don't eat into your profit each time you do up the place.

CHAPTER 24
STORAGE PLACE RENTAL

Make money by renting the space left over in your home! The concept of collaborative economy is growing every day and who wins is us, ordinary citizens. Sharing private transportation, office space, renting houses and apartments by season, free time exchange and other options are showing that the future is increasingly collective and less individual. But, have you heard the rental of space at home? That's it. The Wistor is a platform recently launched promoting the encounter between people who have space left at home. They are people who need this space to store their belongings, personal belongings, goods, among others.

HOW DOES HOME SPACE RENT WORK?

Those interested in advertising can make empty rooms available; attics, garages and other diverse spaces that are not being occupied but which can be used to store objects. The interested party sees the ad, and the two are put in touch to combine the details. This is an innovative platform that competes directly with services self-storage. That is, those companies that rent sheds for diverse storage. Generally, renting one of these sheds is expensive and is unobjectionable for those who only need a compact space, are moving and cannot shell out large sums.

In addition, the Wistor also lends a helping hand to anyone who has unproductive space at home, apartment, ranch or other places, giving the opportunity to earn extra income without much effort. Small entrepreneurs, shopkeepers and merchants can also benefit from this collaborative system, not having to rent another property for storage. Another great advantage is that the platform allows the spaces available for rent to be found in the vicinity of those who are looking for it.

LESS PAPERWORK AND BUREAUCRACY

Wistor promises a simple and uncomplicated rent, not requiring paperwork or bureaucracies to make room for rent at home. The settlement is done among the stakeholders in the business.

In an interview with Exame magazine, the co-founder of the Franz Bories platform explains that the site receives 15% commission on the rents on a monthly basis. This fee includes legal support if there are problems such as disagreements and disagreements between who offers the space and who rents, in addition to insurance in the amount of up to $ 1,000.00 in case of damage to the stored objects. According to him, Wistor still does not offer insurance against theft and other contingencies, but this is an idea that is being developed and probably should be put into practice in the future through a partnership with an insurance company.

HOW TO ADVERTISE AN AVAILABLE SPACE AND EARN EXTRA INCOME (EXAMPLE: WISTOR)?

1. Enter the platform wistor.com and enter the region where your space is.

2. Specify the period when your space will be available (days, months, etc.) and also the time the renter will have access to it;

3. Set a value per square meter. Make sure the price is on the average of the other ads;

4. Use photos! Pictures are very important at the time of the renter's decision!

5. And do not forget, the more information you make available, the more chances you'll have to close a good deal!

By the way, it will be great if you already know about real estate insurance. If not, then do read up.

CHAPTER 25
VACATION PROPERTY BROKER

Here's a bit of history to consider. Less than 20 years ago, brokers only relied on the phone, shoe sole, and newspaper ads to capture clients and real estate. Presentations, tables and simulations of proposals were delivered on paper only, in person or via mail. The most ease one had was being able to use the old fax machine to send some document. Fortunately, this reality has changed radically, and all needs of customer service have come to rely on technological resources, which were further favored by the popularization of social networks and the possibility of access to information from mobile devices.

With this, today, as in any segment, the real estate market and the internet have become inseparable. And so has the role of a vacation property broker changed drastically.

And as I have mentioned above for various roles, mentioning a few tips here to make the best use of this relationship and be a successful vacation property broker.

1 - GAIN KNOWLEDGE
Make no mistake that knowledge is a solid foundation for success to be achieved. In fact, you may even be a good connoisseur of the various features that the internet is able

to offer. But do you know all the tools so well that you know how to exploit them to the fullest?

Therefore, look for courses and training aimed at the techniques of using the tools that the internet offers.

2 - SEGMENT YOUR TARGET AUDIENCE
The possibilities of the internet are unlimited. However, in such a large and comprehensive universe, if you do not create specific foci, and especially in the sector of vacation properties, you may get very limited results if they arise. Therefore, it is critical that you map out the profiles of the types of audiences you want to meet and design your other actions accordingly. For example, differentiate your actions and campaigns between people who want to rent for shorter intervals, and those who want to rent it for longer intervals.

3 - CREATE A PAGE ON FACEBOOK AND RELEASE IT
It is not unusual for the broker to have a personal profile on Facebook and, through it, among the photos of the weekend, publishes real estate offers or needs funding. If you act like this, among the friends of the network, eventually you may even find who is buying or selling a property, which does not invalidate the whole initiative. However, you will find much greater success if you professionalize your presence on Facebook. To do so, start by creating a page where only information and images related to your real estate business will be published. To get started, invite your Facebook friends to enjoy the page, but

do not be alone in it. After all, 1,000 or 2,000 users represent success in promoting the page to your direct audience, but it does not represent that you will succeed in business.

So, invest in the promotion of the page, seeking users and potential renters beyond your audience. Make this investment rationally by setting a budget that is compatible with your ability to pay and distribute the promotion amount very carefully.

4 - INVEST IN THE DISCLOSURE OF THE OFFERS AND THE DEMANDS

Part of that budget of disclosure of the page or an exclusive amount you must reserve to promote specific offers and demands pertaining to the seasonal nature of the property, for example (off-seasons and on-seasons).

5 - CREATE A WEBSITE

Today's websites are fundamental for someone to be present on the internet consistently. In it, you can not only present your offers and demands but also outline your areas of expertise and professional experience, as well as create a channel of contact with potential buyers and sellers. However, since the first impression is the one that stays, take care to register an easily assimilated domain and to have the site professionally prepared.

Do not forget to integrate your site with Facebook and other social networks, and also take care that it is responsive in order to become visible from all operating systems, considering that today most of the internet access is done through of mobile devices.

6 - HAVE AN EMAIL ACCOUNT WITH THE EXTENSION OF YOUR SITE

Really, it is quite practical to use the free email accounts of Google, Yahoo or Outlook. You can also use a real estate account to which you may be associated. However, considering that you have invested in creating a website, which requires a domain of your own, having an email account of the type "yourname@yourdomain.com" will certainly create a more professional and credible image that will be very favourable to your performance to the clientele.

7 - INVEST IN GOOGLE ADWORDS

Investing in Google Adwords greatly improves the visibility of your site, which can appear in ads on other sites. Include that investment in your total budget, which is relatively cheaper than the forms of marketing and advertising of traditional campaigns. In addition, from this strategy, you can target the audience you want to reach.

8 - CREATE A CHANNEL ON YOUTUBE

A survey by Ibope found that 64% of people looking for real estate access YouTube for information. This number makes it very interesting to maintain a channel on the site, where you can display videos of your offers and the differences with regards to parameters and changes which keep happening to the property. Eventually, if you are a good communicator, you can even produce videos with different information about the real estate market, which will be useful for generating access and attracting customers.

SECTION

THREE

LEARNING SKILL BASED METHODS TO EARN PASSIVE INCOME

CHAPTER 26
STANDARD RATE AND DATA SERVICE
(SRDS)

Today, a lot is said about performance, scalability, process automation, and business productivity issues. For those who live the day to day life of a CIO in large companies, or closely follow what happens in the IT areas of these companies, this becomes even more evident. We are becoming increasingly concerned about what needs to be done to reduce accounts and increase performance. Delivering results faster by spending less, without hampering processes, increasing productivity whenever possible, is a constant goal.

To meet the new demands more quickly, the tools and services related to cloud computing have been gaining evidence and relevance over time. A good example of this is the Software as a Service (SaaS) concept. Since the arrival of solutions based on this concept, many attitudes in IT management began to be questioned, which paved the way for its constant evolution.

SaaS consists of providing one or more software typically over the Internet in the service model, usually paid monthly, and its cost can vary by several factors, such as number of users, resources used, among others. See below for the best benefits that SaaS usage can add to you and your team:

1. REDUCING LICENSE COSTS

Because they are almost always based on periodic payments, the high cost for software licenses is set aside. These monthly payments (also with other options such as quarterly, half-yearly and yearly payments) are more accessible than the old licenses for product versions, as well as allowing better control over the long term, without any surprises in financial planning.

2. REDUCING INFRASTRUCTURE AND MAINTENANCE

Because they are hosted in the cloud publicly or privately to your company, using SaaS enables you to reduce your infrastructure to the fullest. More servers are taking up space, consuming energy, demanding hours of maintenance and care from your IT staff.

3. FOCUS ON YOUR BUSINESS

When choosing a service, you do not have to worry so much about your internal infrastructure, periodic and emergency maintenance, backups of your data, and manual software upgrades when using SaaS. You and your entire team gain more time to focus on the daily work and knowledge in the evolution of your own business.

4. GREAT PARTNER OF TI BIMODAL

TI Bimodal is a rapidly growing trend, as it allows the union of two IT models to achieve more agility and innovation without leaving aside the solidity and responsible evolution within the business environment.

5. DATA SECURITY AND AVAILABILITY ASSURANCES

When adopting a SaaS, you should be aware that a lot of your company information is going to a server in the cloud, such as communication, tasks, plans, projects, and so on. But whenever the doubts come up and make you question the whole process, remember all the work you and your team had to perform and maintain backups of your entire structure, without error-freeness and setbacks. Now think that this is the responsibility of the provider of that service.

6. ACCESS ANYTIME, ANYWHERE

One of the basic principles of SaaS is that it is accessible anytime, anywhere. Through a browser and an internet connection, its users have easy access at any time, making it an important differential that allows more mobility, agility and practicality for all employees inside and outside the business environment.

7. CONSTANT UPDATES

Your system update issues end here. No worries about operating system versions and minimum workstation requirements so that new versions of your software can be installed and working properly. In SaaS, the update in question happens on the provider side, and you do not have to worry - no downloads of endless patches and time-consuming installations.

Following this list of advantages, we can safely say that SaaS has come to stay in the IT market.

CHAPTER 27
WRITER (GHOSTWRITING)

If you love working with words, then one of the ways on how to make money on the internet is by becoming a freelance copywriter. Even if you do not have experience in this activity, you can start without major problems. And already get to get some money from it. The first thing you need to think about is a niche and decide what type of writing you will use. For example:

There are a bunch of contents, almost infinite, which you can write and specialize. Your main decision will be what kind of writer you will be and exactly what you are going to work with. Once you've decided, it's time to start creating some samples of your work and spreading them over the net. Some of the most popular channels for doing this are LinkedIn and Medium. Both platforms are great places to show your full potential.

If you are already starting to get started, we recommend some content with extra tips on what you can do as a freelance writer.

CHAPTER 28
TRANSLATION SERVICE
(BACKSEAT TRANSLATOR)

This profile is pretty self-explanatory in terms of the roles and responsibilities one would have to undertake if trying this. I think the more important and more necessary thing is to actually understand the environment the freelance translator will find in the current translation market.

This will also be useful to prepare an efficient business plan since, as in any type of business, planning must always be the first step for those who start some economic activity. Therefore, the topics discussed below will help demystify, un-complicate and broaden the view on the positioning of the translation business for freelancers in the market.

To begin with, I must make it clear that the translation service should only be done by people who completely dominate two or more languages. This is also a complex activity because translators should learn to deal with situations that make service delivery even more difficult. Among the situations that the freelancer translator will find are problems with source text and language problems. The most frequent problems with the source text are incomplete texts, non-digitized texts, poorly printed texts, poorly scanned texts, Poorly written texts, lack of references, quotes without the original text, changes in the text during the translation process.

Already with the language, you can come across the following situations: language too technical, literary texts written in a very old language, texts with strong regionalist influences, dialects, unexplained abbreviations, own names, names of organizations, slang and jargon, idiomatic expressions, redundant phrases, language conventions and agreements and graphical accentuations.

Any of these situations, if not very well observed, organized and adapted by the translator, could interfere in the target language and the interpretation that the readers will have of the message of the translated text.

Another highlight among the language problems most faced by translators euphonic and dissonance, cultural characteristics, poetic texts, puns, specific idiomatic properties, rhymes, common terms in one region but unknown in another (for these cases it is necessary a clear explanation of what one wants to convey), and false cognates, which are similar words in two languages, but which have the different meaning, for example: the word "scene." In Portuguese, it is a reference to the space occupied by the stage of a theatre; In Spanish, it means "dinner."

TRANSLATION AS A PROFESSION

There is no need for proof to certify the translator's ability. But of course, the market is not silly and will always select the best prepared to meet your needs. The lack of regulation, in general, makes it easier for freelancers to access the market, who only need to master their native language very well and at least have an intermediate / advanced level in the foreign language.

THE PROFILE OF THE TRANSLATOR IN THE RECENT HISTORY

But to understand the role of translation with a more modern view, we will have to focus on the recent history of the profession and retreat only seven or eight decades ago. In this way, we will be able to understand how the freelancers' routine in the translation market was in the early 20th century.

At that time, for example, a translator of scientific literature was probably a teacher or scientist, almost always retired, who had vast knowledge in its area of expertise. Only the experience of having worked and studied his whole life on a particular branch was already the guarantee that his translation would be faithful and reliable. In this case, the translator was something like a traveling library that, in addition to its native language, dominated one or more foreign languages. If we consider that at that time there were not many language schools, nor computers, let alone translation tools like Google Translator, we will conclude that being a translator meant to belong to a profession of the highest level, restricted to a select group of professionals specialized and experienced, who translated specific texts, being limited only to their areas of activity. For example, only a doctor could translate a text about medicine; or, only a philosopher would faithfully translate a text of philosophy.

Nowadays, anyone with a computer that is curious and who likes to research can be a translator, achieving levels of fidelity and reliability of translation equal to and even superior to those pioneers of the beginning of the last century. The great advantages of modern translators are: the ease of access to infinite information, through literature and the Internet; intensive language courses, increasingly fast and of acceptable quality; computers and translation software that streamline and facilitate the process; and online communities of freelance translators who help each other, solving each other's doubts and difficulties.

Today, virtually anyone with an acceptable domain of at least two languages can translate any type of text, even without ever having contact with a specific area of the market.

THE TRANSLATION MARKET

I will conclude with some basic information on the translation market, under the following aspects: Literary, technical, media and journalistic translations so that you get the basic idea of how translations work in these verticals.

LITERARY TRANSLATION

Foreign authors, once unknown, are successful and stick their titles among the world bestsellers. Result: there is a growing need to translate these titles into several languages around the globe. One of the great examples of this is the abysmal number of books put up for sale without any mediation from the former publishers. There have been cases of authors, almost anonymous, and ignored by large publishers, who make thousands of dollars monthly by selling their books and e-books on retail Internet sites like Amazon.com, for example.

TECHNICAL

Technical translation currently accounts for approximately 90% of translations. Usually, they are manuals of products and machines; texts related to medicine; administration, economics and finance; electronics or mechanics in general.

MEDIA TRANSLATION

It has to do with subtitling of audio and video. Just to give an example, it is known that this is a shortage in the market, due to the lack of specific courses and training.

TRANSLATION JOURNALISM

Again, globalization. In this case, and in general, it is the journalists themselves who carry out the translations, adapting the world news to the local language.

CHAPTER 29
FREELANCING

Let's face it, starting your own agency is a little intimidating, and not everyone is confident to do it straight away. Once you have your own team of highly skilled professionals put together, you may want to try out something that does not involve that much of a risk and will still get you paid. Thankfully, there are tons of freelancing websites like Upwork out there that allow you to sell your skills to potential business owners for a fair price.

There are a lot of benefits to working on these websites, and one of them is that you have a minimum investment in terms of space. You can also learn from your mistakes that you make as a freelancer and use those lessons for when you start planning your own agency. Freelancing is great because it gives you the opportunity to work with people all across the globe, and this helps you to understand market trends everywhere. The more time you spend freelancing, the stronger your profile gets, and this makes it easier for you to start your business with confidence.

At the end of the day, your main goal is to establish your own social media marketing agency, so whichever way you get there, it is always going to be something that you want to achieve. The reason it makes more sense for you to practice before you actually take the plunge is that this helps you to recognize what your weak points are and it helps you to work on them before you actually start investing money in the business and then try to rectify the problem.

FOUR

LEARNING OFFLINE METHODS TO EARN PASSIVE INCOME

CHAPTER 30
PHOTOGRAPHY ROYALTY
(STOCK PHOTOGRAPHER)

The search for how to make money with photography grows with each passing day. Making money with photography can be the perfect work option, with no fixed schedule and high profitability, of course, for this you need to learn how to make money with photography, from the option clichés like weddings, birthdays and graduations to the sale of images on the Internet.

Currently, the list of possibilities to make money with photography is great, and the investment is affordable, so if you are looking for how to make money with photography, this content is perfect! I've done a search and reviewed the most promising ways and ideas to make money with photography

ANIMAL PHOTOGRAPHY

The pet sector has been growing for years, in 2018 the percentage was 9%. If you want to learn how to make money with photography and have ease with pets here is an excellent option to make money with photos. The focus should be on investing in good scenarios and characterizing pets, like the work of photographing babies. To start in this niche and to make money with photography the investment is very accessible, basically the professional equipment of photographers, scenarios and some clothes for the animals.

MAKE MONEY WITH PHOTOGRAPHY IN EVENTS

Events such as weddings, graduations, birthdays, and parties, in general, can be highly lucrative for photographers. The problem faced is a large number of professionals and mainly companies responsible for organizing the entire event, consequently providing their own photographers. The good news is that it is an option to make money with highly profitable photography, perhaps the highest paid, and you can charge values over R $ 1,000 per event.

BABY PHOTOGRAPHY

Babies are the perfect audience for those who want to make money with photography and at the same time spend little and have a loyal clientele. The photos start already in the first months, and every year the parents come back, again, to the photographer to take photos. Normally, photographs of babies remain until the age of 4, maintaining a good stabilization of clients.

Just like in photographs of pets, this case requires nice scenery, toys, and different outfits to make the babies even cuter and would guarantee an eternal memory for their parents. The marketing of the work is fundamental to make money with photographing babies, and a good form of publicity is the use of social networks like Instagram and Facebook, which are cheap, allow information sharing and are frequently accessed by the parents.

PHOTOS FOR E-COMMERCE SITES AND OTHER SITES

E-commerce websites need high-resolution, quality photos that interpret the context. For example, the images of products sold to the store should arouse the visitor's buying interest, so its importance. Studies already indicate that images in the products offered significantly increase the purchase rate, especially when they are of good quality.

CREATING A FASHION BLOG OR PHOTOGRAPHY

The photography professional can work with digital marketing and have their own business. Blogs of photography and fashion, for example, usually have many accesses and with that, it is possible to monetize.

PHOTO SERVICES WITH DRONES

The use of Drones is on the rise in many professions. In photography and video recording, you can get excellent results from images, provided you have quality equipment.

Aerial event photography is one of the people's favorite requests for photographers, and many are failing to take advantage of this opportunity. Invest now in a drone and equipment to shoot and record videos, it will surely be a differential in your profession, and you can increase your income with photography.

SALE OF PHOTOS - STOCK PHOTOS

Do you like to take photos professionally and have creativity? Did you know that there are sites where images can be made available for sale in a simple, practical and highly profitable way? Also known as a Stock photographer, it is one that assembles a vast repertoire of images and makes them available in marketplaces, that is, platforms of sale of images.

In these platforms, the interested ones pay the value by the image and use, avoiding complications with copyrights. Good examples of marketplaces to sell the photographs are Photodune, Fotolia, Bigstock and Shutterstock.

CHAPTER 31
DIVIDEND INCOME
(DIVIDEND-PAYING STOCKS)

Many investors say this a lot of times, "I have R $ X.000, is it a good idea to invest in the stock market?"

The first thing you should know is yes; it is possible to make money on the stock exchange. This market offers many earning opportunities, with several examples of success, such as those achieved by fund managers. Managers who have profited more than 30% in the last 24 months - which is a much better performance than savings and much higher than the Ibovespa, lost -2% in the same period.

In times of markets in crisis, stop and think: how much was your profitability in the last 12 months? Did you earn $ 200 for every $ 1000 invested? It's not that easy. The stock exchange is not that easy. Many investors are tempted to "make a fortune in the stock market," start investing on their own, do not know enough and end up coming out worse than they entered.

An alternative that I recommend is not going into the stock market alone. Instead, invest through an investment fund that has behind it a professional manager who will study the market and invest your money for you.

Hire a Professional. Unlike many investors imagine, having a professional manager looking after your money is very easy, simple and cheap, in addition to being more profitable most of the time.

Managers have access to information that the investor alone does not have. They use modern analysis and simulation tools, as well as having a team 100% focused on the search for the best opportunities in the market. "But I have a profit by investing alone!" Many investors go so far as to delude themselves that the only thing that matters is having a positive profitability. In fact, the important thing is to compare your profitability with the market as a whole. What I mean is that it's no use thinking you're a great investor if you've earned 10% in the year, while the market has risen by 15%.

I also want to use this opportunity to tell you about the advantages of a professional manager. He offers several advantages compared to venturing alone on the stock exchange.

1. CLEAR OBJECTIVE
The manager already has the pre-determined rules about what the fund can and cannot do, ensuring much more security for investors who apply money.

2. OPPORTUNISTIC AND DYNAMIC STRATEGY

This is the main highlight and difference of the fund compared to other products on the market. Through a dynamic and opportunistic strategy, the professional managers (example: JGP Equity Works) operate by buying and selling according to market movements. With this agility, they are able to take advantage of the best opportunities of the moment and have great capacity of protection of capital in low moments.

3. WELL-DEFINED RISK RULES

The investment fund has clear risk exposure criteria; it ensures that the manager does not take more risk than it should. This is very rare among individual investors since it is often quite complicated to calculate and determine the risk of a particular transaction.

4. 100% FOCUSED ON STOCKS

This condition guarantees that the fund manager will always be attentive to the stock exchange, seeking to determine what the best actions for each moment are.

CHAPTER 32
COMMODITIES TRADING

Binary Trading continues to grow in popularity as the industry has witnessed an increase in the number of traders each year. However, traders have to rely on a certain level of skill to be successful in trading binary options. Your success depends on choosing the right assets to trade, deciding how much to invest, determining the periods you want to use for analysis, and in what direction they want to bet.

If you are a beginner trader in binary options and want to be successful at it, then you need to realize that there is a lot to learn. One of the most important things you should keep in mind as a beginner trader is that you should be very patient and use a strategic approach if you are looking to earn profits consistently in your trading of binary options. You should not let your emotions keep you from giving your best, and you should not stray from your trading strategy.

Binary options traders do not need to buy the actual asset. Let's look at a typical example of binary trading. Suppose you decide to create trading based on the future value of gold, where you need to determine if the price of gold will fall or rise during a stipulated period. You do not have to buy any gold bar for this transaction, because the only thing you need is to put money in your forecast and wait for the results.

Because binary options are extremely simple to understand and negotiate, they soon have become one of the most popular platforms when it comes to financial trading. These options trades give traders the opportunity to make quick gains that are determined by the type of asset you choose and by choosing the direction in trading binary options. To make a profit using binary options, it all boils down to correctly determining the price movement of a given market or asset over a stipulated time.

One of the main differences when it comes to traditional trading and binary options trading is that a trader will lose 100% of his investment if he misses the prognosis in binary trading, while he will probably withhold some of his investment when trading in the traditional market, although the asset acquired may have depreciated significantly.

If you want to be successful in trading binary options, it is important that you take the time to educate yourself about trading binary options before you get seriously involved. We have already made it clear that trading binary options involve speculating on the value of a particular asset over a stipulated time. When a trader decides that the underlying asset is going to go up, he goes ahead and buys an 'UP' option. If the trader believes that the underlying asset will fall, he will buy a 'DOWN' option.

For the trader to make money from the 'UP' transaction, the price of the underlying asset must exceed the strike price by the due date. For the trader to make money with the 'DOWN', then the price of the underlying asset should be lower than the strike price by the due date. The strike price, also known as the strike price, is determined by the value level of the underlying asset when the trader buys the binary option. The trader will be able to find out the strike price, expiration date, risk, and payment before entering the transaction.

After the transaction is completed, trading is started and there is nothing else the trader can do except wait for the expiration of the term and then see the end result.

WHAT ARE BINARY OPTIONS STRATEGIES?

These are the broad strategies which one needs to keep in mind:

1. TREND CAPTURE

When the term 'trend capture' is used in the context of binary options, it is important to note that it is not being used to pinpoint trends that last the last two weeks or months but is highlighting mini-trends that have occurred in the hours or minutes. If you want to be a successful binary options trader, careful monitoring of breaking news is critical so you can take advantage of these trends and become successful in trading binary options.

2. REVERSION STRATEGY

Binary options traders have the option of combining the above trend capture strategy with the reversal strategy we will explain below. To implement the two strategies together, it will be necessary for the trader to have a certain amount of technical know-how to succeed with this dual strategy. All trends tend to reverse over time. Traders who are well versed in the industry can use charts to determine with a certain level of accuracy when a trend is about to reverse. They can profit from this trend when it begins a reversal of direction and reverse.

WHAT ARE THE BENEFITS?

There are a number of benefits in investing in binary options when compared to investing in more traditional trading methods.

SPEED

Investors who follow the traditional trading market route realize that it can take weeks, months and even years before they make any profit from their investment. However, trading binary options gives traders quicker results, although there are some binary options that allow traders to trade on a long-term basis.

POTENTIAL PROFITS & RETURNS

Unlike traditional investments, binary options give traders the opportunity to make potential profits of up to 80% while trading in the short term. Although the return on investment is extremely high, it is important to note that it is also extremely risky. If an investor invests $ 100 in a short-term binary options deal and hits, he may receive an additional $ 80. However, if he makes a mistake, he may end up losing his $ 100.

GLOBAL MARKET ACCESS

Binary options traders have access to global markets and the opportunity to choose from hundreds of underlying stock-market assets around the world.

GETTING PROFITS FROM UP AND DOWN MARKETS

One of the great advantages of trading binary options is that traders can make money regardless of current market conditions as they have the option of selecting stocks when the market is going up, down or even walking laterally.

You can read at greater lengths about trading from a number of sources, but what is more important according to me, are the tips mentioned below:

SELECT A GOOD BINARY OPTIONS BROKER

The most important advice any binary options trader needs is to make sure you have chosen the correct binary options broker when you begin. A good broker with a solid reputation in the market will know how to do your job and can make all the difference in the way you perform with your trading of binary options.

DIVERSIFY YOUR TRADING

The number of online binary options brokers has grown significantly in recent years, thanks to the increase in the number of binary options traders. While this gives binary option traders a wide range of options when it comes to selecting the binary options broker, it can also be a tricky task as it can be difficult to decide which brokerage is right for you.

ENJOY THE BONUSES

When you are starting with trading binary options, you should make the most of the number of sign-up bonuses that are offered to new traders. These bonuses are provided in an effort to get new binary option traders and are credited to the trader's account after the completion of the registration process. Traders can use these special bonuses as a protection against their real money traders, and to increase their chances of making a profit on their first trading.

EARLY RELEASE NEGOTIATIONS

When you start trading with binary options, you will find that sometimes you will have an option known as an early exit option in some of your dealings. This is a very complicated offer because you can eliminate the risk by going out early, but on the other hand, if you stay, there is a possibility that your transaction will perform better if you stay through the entire previous trading period. If you decide to take the early exit option, you will earn a lower profit, not the full amount you were guaranteed within the stipulated trading period.

AVOID TIPS AND RUMORS

As you continue to trade with binary options, you will find a lot of information on your way, offering you a wide range of tips and assertions that will give you a so-called advantage when it comes to trading options. Keep in mind that when it comes to trading binary options, there is no guarantee that any strategy will work all the time. Your best bet is to invest time to do an in-depth market analysis and then make a decision based on the information you have researched and bet on a negotiation. This is the best way to increase the likelihood of you profiting from trading binary options.

On top of all this, to be a successful professional in binary options, it is critical that you control your emotions. You need to be able to manage your ups and downs, and not negotiate when you feel emotionally disturbed as this will likely have a negative impact on your trading.

HOW MUCH MONEY CAN YOU EARN THROUGH BINARY OPTIONS TRADING

While most financial products tend to be a bit too complicated for the average person, binary options are based on a yes / no decision, making it one of the financial products simpler to negotiate. Dealers can get between 70% and 90% of their trading profits, depending on the online binary options trading platform they choose, the assets they select, and the time frames they choose. Most binary options traders prefer to choose an online binary options trading platform that allows them to bet on trades that have a very short expiration period. This allows these traders to cash in on their transactions within minutes. Although it sounds too good to be true, it is important for traders to understand that there is a mathematical composition associated with trading binary options and it becomes easier for a trader to be consistently successful when he understands how this mathematical composition operates.

The main formula of these compound returns is to constantly increase the profits of the transactions while the binary options are negotiated. The easiest way to explain this is to use an example. Let's assume you make a $ 2000 deposit into your account and then use 5% of that balance to open a deal on your binary options trading platform, where the profit is 70%. If your forecast is correct and you make a profit from trading, your payment will be $ 170; where $ 100 is your bet money and $ 70 is your profit. Once the composite return principle applies, the trader will have to invest the full amount, that is, $ 170 in his next trading and if he finishes hitting again, he will receive $ 289.

CHAPTER 33
FOREIGN LANGUAGE BUSINESS

Every parent knows the importance of mastering foreign languages for the future of their child. Due to this fact, many parents have already thought about the case or have already put their children into language courses. Nowadays, there is still one more facility: the partnerships between language schools/individuals and educational institutions.

HOW IT WORKS

Partnerships between language schools/individuals and educational institutions can start with the interest of the educational institution or language schools / individuals. Working together, their teachers, coordinators, principals, and other academic members set up a contract, think through methodologies, adapt their own school environment, and more to better language learning.

But the courses taught by their language counterpart do not work like any class. Firstly, you should do the leveling of the students, which will define their class (as if it were in normal formation, in which age does not define its class, but it's level in the defined language).

The methodology is also a bit different, such as lessons to learn pronunciation by audio or movies. This cooperation between the traditional school and the language course has many benefits.

BENEFITS FOR PARENTS
This partnership provides your child with greater security and comfort, since lessons can be taught in the school's own environment. The child having language classes in the school itself also allows a greater saving in extra expenses, such as the transportation used to follow up course, for example.

BENEFITS FOR THE CHILDREN
Your child will efficiently learn the chosen language, one of the most basic benefits. There is also greater ease with foreign language classes per se, because of the already familiar school environment, which gives your child greater confidence (he feels less embarrassed, for example, being able to develop further).

WHAT THE EDUCATIONAL INSTITUTION IMPROVES
With an increasingly competitive education-related market, having a prominent differential can make the school stand out. Providing parents with a monthly fee for cheaper courses and ensuring the safety of the child is certainly a great attraction for new students.

WHAT GAIN IN PARTNERSHIPS BETWEEN LANGUAGE SCHOOLS AND INSTITUTIONS
Bringing language courses to an educational institution will attract new students accurately. Be it for the monthly tuition discounts, or for the greater security of the parents (who did not want their children to travel the school-

course, for example) and more. And the students in the partnership classes can indicate the language school for acquaintances, which attracts even more students.

Given all these benefits, it is possible to understand why the partnership between educational institutions and a language school can be so rewarding. It is almost like a guarantee of a successful income generating service, which is making and filling an important gap in the education sector.

CHAPTER 34
CAR RENTAL

This is another one of those profiles where I would like to explain the need which exists in the current society for car rentals and why the number of people opting for it will keep on increasing continuously. Currently, having a new car in the garage is not necessarily just a matter of hobby or vanity. In fact, the car, much more than a simple vehicle of locomotion, has become an alternative for those who want to increase their monthly income. But is the best way to enjoy the benefits of owning a new car is by getting one? Or is it more advantageous to ride with a zero car, hiring a car rental plan?

Lately, much has been discussed about the advantages or disadvantages of having a car by subscription, a service that is being made available by the rental companies and that, little by little, is gaining strength in the country. In order for you to draw your own conclusions, I am going to bring to you the possible benefits or losses in choosing to buy a new vehicle or joining the vehicle subscription service.

Most of the vehicles on the streets are in service. The tendency to turn the car into an extra source of income is getting stronger among people. This is easily proven if we consider that most of the vehicles on the streets are in the service of applications, such as Uber, among others. One of the great balconies of this type of transport is that, when calling the driver, it is necessary to inform the origin and destination addresses of the trip.

The convenience of being able to drink in the ballad and not having to worry about driving on the way back home also makes the car application service very much in demand. And for the driver too, there are many advantages! The possibility of it deciding how much money you want to earn, since the more customers you get, the more profitable the business is, it's a big draw, for example. That is, the driver is the one who makes the profit itself!

And the value of all the trips of the week that the app driver performs will be deposited into your checking account or savings on a single weekly deposit. With all these advantages, for drivers and users, and the consequent adherence of people to transportation applications, you may be thinking that the demand for vehicles has decreased, have not you?

The flexibility in the use of the vehicle influences the demand for vehicles in the automotive market. Contrary to what one might imagine, the demand for cars in the country did not decline with the emergence of the new mode of transportation by application. Research has pointed to a considerable increase in demand for new cars in recent years. The flexibility in the use of the vehicle, therefore, directly influences the growth of the demand for vehicles in the automotive market. That is, there is a greater number of people using vehicles, either to move with more agility and safety or for comfort or work.

WHAT DOES ONE MEAN BY OWNING A CAR BY SIGNATURE?

The pay-per-car service consists of offering monthly or annual car rental plans.

Already very common in the United States and Europe, the option to hire a service of signing new cars is also becoming an accessible reality in the market. The service consists of offering monthly or annual car rental plans. These plans are offered by insurers, rental companies and even by mobile applications. That way, you can ride with zero worries about financing or any other way of acquiring the vehicle. You also will not need to stress about the payment of insurance, IPVA, licensing, or even periodic reviews and maintenance of the property.

In addition, it is possible for the user to leave the car at the time of signing the contract. This is very important since some people need to use the car on the same day as the agreement.

To make it cheaper for a car by subscription, it is possible that more people from the same family use the vehicle, which is a" hand in the wheel."

However, as this type of service is new in the market, it is necessary that we make a deeper assessment, because it is fundamental, for those who work with the car and take their livelihood, knowing which of the options to maintain a vehicle is the most profitable. With that in mind, I will compare the advantages of owning a new car by subscription and purchasing a new car through financing (the vehicle's most common vehicle acquisition mode in the country).

The fact that the user of the vehicle does not have to worry about the rush and the expenses related to the payment of taxes is already quite attractive! As we have seen above, the car service subscription offers numerous user facilities.

For example, the fact that the user of the vehicle does not need to worry about the rush and the expenses related to the payment of taxes (IPVA, Licensing) is an attractive and so much, right? Another advantage is that the maintenance and the necessary revisions to the good functioning of the vehicle are all on account of the company that provides the car, that is, the user is also free of the concern with these values. In addition, the instructor says that you do not need to stress about the maintenance of the car, because it is attended with agility anywhere. And finally, another attractive feature of car subscription service is the ease of leasing.

CHAPTER 35
RENT YOUR CAR FOR AD SPACE

Have you ever thought about turning your car costs into profit without making any extra effort? With platforms like Carlicity, this is possible, and - to earn extra money - you simply follow your routine as usual. These are a meeting platform for advertising cars with their advertisers. This means that you register your vehicle and inform your normal routine, and the platform selects some advertisers that fit your offer.

If you accept any of these offers, your car will be affixed, and you will receive money monthly, according to the signed contract. There is no cost to the owner of the car, and just drive normally on the itinerary indicated.

To participate, you simply register on the platform, register the car you have, with the brand, model, year, color, and the itinerary you usually do, as well as your schedules. Whenever you find a demand that complies with your routine, the platforms will advise you, telling you what the monthly offer paid by the advertiser company is. If you agree, the advertiser company is responsible for all the costs of bonding and care, and you only need to direct and receive the money at the end of the month. If you do not want to promote that ad, just decline the offer and wait for the next one.

HOW MUCH DO I GET WITH THE STICKER?

The amount you receive depends, of course, on the city, the type of advertisement, the type of car, and the itinerary that you travel through. In general, the factor that most influences the value received is the path travelled. That means that the more miles traveled daily, the higher the amount received at the end of the month, according to the combined service across the platform. In addition, various companies include special contract offers such as fuel supply, recurring washes, or other advantages that are interesting to both the driver and the advertiser.

FINAL

WORDS

I hope you enjoyed checking out the various methods you can earn good money through passive income! While this may all seem very lucrative and interesting, it's essential you find your calling and stick to something you know will work well for you. Trial and error is part of the game, but make sure you experiment with the ones you're passionate about!

Finally, if you found this book useful in any way, a review on Amazon is always appreciated!

JONATHAN FITZPATRICK

SIGN UP!

Visit our website:

WWW.JONATHANFITZPATRICKAUTHOR.COM

and enter you email address to receive exclusive bonus contents related to the updates of this book and find out everything about Jonathan Fitzpatrick's new publications, launch offers and other exclusive promotions!

JONATHAN FITZPATRICK'S
OTHER PUBLICATIONS

available at
amazon

AMAZON FBA MASTERY COACHING

THE DEFINITIVE GUIDE TO LEARN THE SECRET WAY TO SELL FULFILLMENT BY AMAZON

HOW TO LAUNCH A PRIVATE LABEL AND EARN SIX FIGURES OF PASSIVE INCOME IN AN EASY STEP-BY-STEP METHOD FROM TOTAL BEGINNERS TO REALLY ADVANCED

What is Amazon FBA? What can I do with FBA? Is it as challenging as my colleagues at work keep saying? Is it worth the trouble? Depending on how well you know or understand Fulfillment By Amazon, these are some of the questions you may have asked yourself. Well, look no further because this book is the ultimate compass t making money, and possibly a lot of it, online through FBA.

It matters not where at what point this book finds you. If you have made the conscious decision to see positive change in life, then with this book there is no looking back. Take a deep breath and believe that the transformation is already set in motion. Frankly speaking, if you are already this far, the ball is definitely already rolling. For what it is worth, I do believe in you.

Inside you will find valuable, and quite possibly life-saving, information designed to let you first understand the basic principles of the journey you are embarking on. You will learn what essentially is the premise of human psychology and the dark approach to it as well. Furthermore, you will delve into in depth summation of the techniques. With each technique is a concise elaboration of the approach and impact. At your beck and call, you will have a priceless treasure that is meant to propel you to gaining insight into the hidden secrets of the psychological world.

You being here has unequivocally taken a lot of gut and conviction. The biggest hurdle is ever getting started and it is the stumbling block for many individuals. Boldly take that first step. Do not let yourself get complacent. Get started by buying this book today!

Inside you will find:

- The blueprint to building an FBA business and empire.

- Guidelines on how to get started with Amazon FBA in 2019.

- Guidelines on products, listing, and shipping.

- Gaining traction and feedback on your products.

- Strategies and techniques for gaining an advantage over your competitors.

And more...

available at

RENTAL PROPERTY INVESTING

SECRETS OF A REAL ESTATE BUILDING EMPIRE

available at
amazon

PRINCIPLES TO MAKE 7 FIGURES OF A PASSIVE INCOME ESTABLISHING A REAL ESTATE INVESTMENT EMPIRE

You are looking for something. Something is out there waiting for you, you just know it. It is your salvation, your saving grace, the path to the lifestyle you have always known you were born to live. The question is: what is IT?

IT is real estate rental property and it is the key to your future as a smart business owner who knows what they want and goes out to get it. It is the excitement of finding the perfect rental property for the perfect tenant and bringing in the cash to find the next perfect property and begin all over again. And this book, *Rental Property Investing: Secrets of a Real Estate Building Empire: Principles to Make 7 Figures of a Passive Income Establishing a Real Estate Investment Empire* is the book that holds the keys to your future. When you follow the steps outlined in this book you will become the real estate rental property investor that you always wanted to be, on your way to living the life you always knew you were meant to live.

You will learn why real estate is the perfect career for anyone who has the passion to be successful at it. You will learn how to locate good properties for rental properties and exactly the steps you need to take to purchase them. You will see the difference between different types of properties and how each one can make you a successful entrepreneur.

We will show you who you need to surround yourself with to make yourself successful. We will discuss ways to buy property when you really don't have the money to spare. And we will discuss whether or not flipping is the way for you to acquire your new rental properties.

Investing in real estate rental property seems scary because buying a house is a big purchase and most people only buy one or two at a time. You want to buy dozens. But this book will show you how it is done and why you don't need to fear the future in your new career. You were meant to do this; you just need to begin.

Above all everything you need to know is explained in words you can understand, with examples where needed. And all the tips and tricks you will need to become successful is right here in this book. This is the book that will lead you to the beginning of your new career, one that will get you to the path take you through the rest of your life.

available at

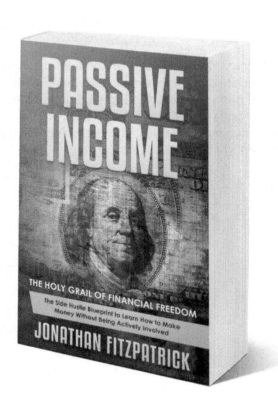

PASSIVE INCOME

THE HOLY GRAIL OF FINANCIAL FREEDOM

available at
amazon

THE SIDE HUSTLE BLUEPRINT TO LEARN HOW TO MAKE MONEY WITHOUT BEING ACTIVELY INVOLVED

You have a regular 9 to 5 job and every month you receive a salary that pays the bills, but in the back of your mind, you have that will to gain a little more. You may want to have a little more freedom to work as you want to, from where you want. Until one fine day, you finally decide to change that reality and put your dreams first. Sounds familiar? Great! In this scenario, the best thing is to invest in any kind of activity that can generate passive income.

This book is the best way for you to learn more about passive income and how it can give you the freedom that you desire. This book will give you all the information you need regarding passive income and how you can go about learning the various techniques. These techniques have been tried and tested by successful entrepreneurs across the world, and you will love the ideas that you will read here. But before you move forward, you need to know what passive income is all about.

What is Passive Income?

Passive income is earned from an activity or an occupation that does not demand continuous "active" work and is still capable of generating income. Passive income activities usually involve a lot of work during the creation process - but once finalized and launched, these activities can generate steady profits for a long time.

A classic example is an online course. You will spend a few weeks or even months creating the site and the material. Then you will not have to work that hard anymore, and you will continue to make a profit. The same goes for a virtual store, with videos and even with books.

With passive income, it is possible to generate money even without working every day - and that is why so many entrepreneurs want to know more about the subject.

With this book, you will learn all the techniques that you need to generate a six-figure income without too much effort from your end. All you need to do is sit back and enjoy your financial freedom.

available at

AMAZON FBA MASTERY COACHING & PASSIVE INCOME

THE HOLY GRAIL OF FINANCIAL FREEDOM

available at

amazon

2 MANUSCRIPTS IN ONE!

AMAZON FBA MASTERY COACHING
THE DEFINITIVE GUIDE TO LEARN THE SECRET WAY TO SELL FULFILLMENT BY AMAZON

HOW TO LAUNCH A PRIVATE LABEL AND EARN SIX FIGURES OF PASSIVE INCOME IN AN EASY STEP-BY-STEP METHOD FROM TOTAL BEGINNERS TO REALLY ADVANCED

&

PASSIVE INCOME
THE HOLY GRAIL OF FINANCIAL FREEDOM

THE SIDE HUSTLE BLUEPRINT TO LEARN HOW TO MAKE MONEY WITHOUT BEING ACTIVELY INVOLVED

available at

JONATHAN
FITZPATRICK

Made in the USA
Coppell, TX
12 April 2020

19762130R00177